Charlie Taylor has been a behavioural specialist for over ten years. He has taught every age group, from nursery to 16-year-olds, working in tough inner city primary and comprehensive schools. He is currently the head teacher of a special school for children with behavioural, emotional and social difficulties in West London. His school has twice received 'outstanding' ratings by Ofsted since he arrived in 2006. He also works as a freelance behaviour consultant, coaching teachers in behaviour management techniques, and holds regular workshops for parents. He lives in London and is married with three immaculately behaved children.

For Lucy

Divas & Door Slammers

The Secrets to Having a Better Behaved Teenager

CHARLIE TAYLOR

Vermilion
LONDON

1 3 5 7 9 10 8 6 4 2

Published in 2010 by Vermilion, an imprint of Ebury Publishing
A Random House Group Company

The Random House Group Limited Reg. No. 954009

Addresses for companies within the Random House Group can be found at www.randomhouse.co.uk

A CIP catalogue record for this book is available from the British Library

The Random House Group Limited supports The Forest Stewardship Council (FSC), the leading international forest certification organisation. All our titles that are printed on Greenpeace approved FSC certified paper carry the FSC logo. Our paper procurement policy can be found at www.rbooks.co.uk/environment

Designed and set by seagulls.net

Printed in the UK by CPI Mackays, Chatham, ME5 8TD

ISBN 9780091924119

To buy books by your favourite authors and register for offers visit www.rbooks.co.uk

contents

SECTION FOUR
Troubleshooting Guide

introduction

Between the ages of 12 and 14, there appears to be an astonishing change in some children. Parents suddenly find their charming, sweet, biddable child becomes, almost overnight, argumentative, uncommunicative, bad-tempered, lazy, messy and disrespectful. For many parents it feels as if a door is closed into their child's world and a different person, with whom they have no relationship, appears. For parents this can feel bewildering, depressing and threatening. '*What did we do? Where did we go wrong?*' they ask themselves, as their teenage daughter storms out of the room for the third time that day, slamming every door she can find on the way up to her bedroom. There can be a huge sense of betrayal and let down as a previously trustworthy son starts to lie about where he has been in the evenings.

Most parents have to deal with the relatively minor irritations of having teenagers in the house as untidiness, disorganisation, an obsession with friends and what they are doing, bizarre fashion sense, appalling musical taste and poor communication all go with the territory. These are an acceptable part of the process as children grow up and away from their parents.

This book is aimed at helping the parents for whom the conflict is beginning to become the mood music of their relationship with their teenager, where there is a frequency and intensity of challenging behaviour that is beginning to fundamentally affect life at home. The most common causes of conflict with teenagers, such as untidiness, often seem trivial in nature, but what is really causing the problem is not the mess, but the consistent refusal of the teenager to accept there is a problem or to do anything about it. This book offers a range of practical solutions to the difficulties with teenagers that have been developed from my many years of working with children with behavioural difficulties.

I often think there is too much focus on teenagers as young adults rather than as children. There are times, particularly with younger teenagers, when their behaviour needs to be contained by authoritative grown ups. By not taking control, we are denying teenagers their right to be children, with all the wonder and excitement that goes with it. There is much talk about children growing up too fast and an expectation that they should be allowed to behave like adults. I don't want to deny the inevitable, gradual separation of children away from their parents or the remarkable maturity that teenagers can often show. However, a lot of teenagers are goofy and hopeless, in a shambling, endearing, childish way. They need lots of love and looking after, rather than being pushed out into the world, expected to cope and then vilified when they don't.

We want teenagers to take responsibility for themselves and their actions, but when they can't or won't, we need to do it for them. By actively guiding children when they need it we can help them to develop their own personalities and values in an atmosphere of support and love and with a safety net that will contain and look after them when things go wrong.

Teenagers can be a joy. They can be independent, enthusiastic, naïve, charming, funny, loving and dynamic. For many children, the teenage years seem to sail by with barely a blip and they turn seamlessly into adults with hardly a stutter on the way. There is a gradual and natural changing of the relationship between parent and child, to parent and adult with a minimum of conflict and distress. What is so frustrating for some parents is that for no obvious reason one or more of their children don't follow this rosy path and the teenage years are riven with conflict and pain.

I have developed the strategies in *Divas and Door Slammers* through my long experience of working with children with behavioural difficulties and their parents. I have taught for 18 years in tough inner-city primary and secondary comprehensive schools and I am currently the head teacher of a school for children with behavioural difficulties in West London. We take the most challenging and socially deprived children who have been excluded from school and aim to turn their behaviour around and get them back into mainstream education. I also run regular training workshops for parents on positive behaviour management and I work with individual parents who are having difficulty with their children.

The first part of the book contains a range of positive strategies that will give parents a framework to use when dealing with any type of behaviour. It opens with a short description of how the mind of a teenager works. New research shows that there are huge changes going on in the wiring of children's brains as they become teenagers and this can lead to much of the moodiness and unpredictability in their behaviour. I then explain how teenagers and parents can get locked into a pattern of action and reaction that ultimately feeds the behaviour. I show how parents will be able to stay calm if they plan how they are going to respond when their teenager misbehaves, making the behaviour less likely to happen next time. Then I look at the importance of using praise with teenagers. Many parents feel as if their teenagers have no interest in what they have to say and find it impossible to praise their children without sounding patronising or causing offence. I will show from my time working with the most disaffected teenagers how the need to be praised never goes away, even for the coolest, hardest-to-get-through-to children. I show parents how to praise teenagers in a way that will be accepted and will lead to dramatic improvements in the child's behaviour. We'll also look at how rewards and punishments can be effectively used to support parents in changing their children's behaviour.

Next there is a chapter on hard cases, to be used in emergencies, when children are beyond their parents' control. My advice in this chapter is to set up a tight programme for managing extreme behaviour, by which parents will regain authority using a strict regime of rewards and sanctions. To be successful, parents will need to show a real desire for things to change and a determination to take charge and realign their relationship with their children.

The strategies laid out in the book will be effective in changing the most difficult behaviour and also help with the lower-level irritations that teenagers can cause. Parents will need to be prepared to be both persistent and consistent in their responses to their children. The outcome will be calmer parents who feel in control, well-managed teenagers who feel contained and safe and households in which conflict becomes the exception rather than the norm.

The last section of the book is a troubleshooting guide containing suggestions for dealing with specific, common issues that arise with teenagers, including homework issues, undesirable friends, sex, drugs and alcohol. Living with teenagers going through a difficult patch can be a hard, soul-destroying experience for parents. Parents can be overwhelmed by a sense of guilt that they have not done a good enough job and that they have failed their children in some way. But take heart. The strategies in this book work with the most challenging teenagers I have come across in my professional life and they will work with yours too.

section one

the teenage landscape

1

understanding teenagers

The teenage world has changed almost beyond recognition in the last ten years. The same excitement, problems and anxieties are still there as they ever were, but these are now over layered by new challenges and opportunities that make life as a teenager both more complicated and more stimulating. The technological revolution of the last decade has meant teenagers can communicate in ways that were unthinkable for their parents. Mobile phones mean that teenagers can contact cheaply whomever they like in complete secrecy from their parents. Gone are the days when teenagers would have to get past the parental gatekeeper of the home phone either to make or receive a call. Stilted, one-sided conversations made in code so they could not be overheard can now be conducted in the privacy of the bedroom or by text.

Computers mean people can report on their lives in real time to their friends and the rest of the world through email and social networking sites. They provide endless opportunities for interest, learning and entertainment, but they are also a window to a more frightening, bleaker landscape. At the click of a mouse young children can watch pornography of the most depraved and shocking nature that wouldn't have been available in the seediest Soho sex shop in the 1990s. Television, once regulated in three or four channels that sent you to bed at midnight, has exploded into a torrent of overwhelming choice at any time of the day or night. The idea of the family sitting round on a Sunday night to watch television together is an archaic, alien concept from another age. The average British household has four television sets and 70 per cent of teenagers have a television in their bedroom.

The sexual revolution that began in the 1960s has entered a new phase. In the last five years there has been a spectacular increase in sexually transmitted disease and the four-fold increase in new cases of HIV and AIDS since 1999 are largely among what was previously considered to be the low risk group of heterosexuals. The message to teenagers is everyone is doing it and if you're not, then you're missing out.

Celebrities have become a new aristocracy in which fame and conspicuous wealth are valued above all else. The chasing of high status and designer labels for everything from handbags to mobile phones has, for some teenagers and adults, become an obsession. Teenage wardrobes groan with piles of barely worn, cheap clothes and yet they still have nothing to wear when they go out. The range of new products is simply staggering and shops dedicated to looking good and stopping the inevitable ravages of age populate every high street.

Teenagers can feel under huge pressure to look beautiful and for most of them there is an unbridgeable gap between their own normal, gawky pubescent bodies that have been a major source of anxiety over the ages, and the images of airbrushed, celebrity perfection they now see every day. The bestselling men's magazine, *Men's Health*, has a picture of a young man on the front cover every month, his muscle-bound body offered as the zenith of beauty for the modern man. Look back to the early James Bond films and you will see Sean Connery, a former body builder and model, looking healthy and well proportioned, but there is no 'six pack' rippling out from his stomach. The benchmark for perfection is higher, and in turn, the money women and men are prepared to spend on cosmetic surgery has increased. While our aspirations have changed, large parts of the food industry are dedicated to producing processed food containing little nutrition but plenty of trans-fats, sugar and salt, which make us want to eat more and more. Add to this the more sedentary lifestyle of so many of our teenagers (why go out into the cold and kick a football about when you can play FIFA World Cup in the comfort of your own home?) and you have an explosion of childhood obesity that will blight the long-term happiness and health of so many of our children.

Schools have become more pressurised places, the government has imposed narrow targets that are supposed to signify educational success and the subsequent stress teachers feel in achieving them is passed straight on to the backs of their pupils. The essential part of education that helps children develop 'character' is often squeezed because it can't be measured and doesn't produce results which show up in league tables.

Many of the issues parents face with teenagers today are the same as they have always been. Conflict, guilt and worry are hardwired into the process of changing from a dependent child to an independent adult. Concerns about teenagers and their behaviour have existed since the first cave man caught his daughter snogging next door's son and realised, to his horror, that his little girl was a sexual being. I think the greatest new challenge for parents, indeed for all of us in the next 20 years, is learning discernment. The overloading of the modern world means electrical stimulation is constant and we have to learn to control it ourselves. The 24/7 media barrage has to be filtered. Later generations will find this easier, as they won't have known anything different, but for now it is going to be a struggle for our children to see new media as a slave, not a master. If you want to see what we're up against, sit on a Mediterranean beach and watch the British bob up from their sun lounger every few minutes when their BlackBerry bleeps with another email from work. Is this what a holiday is supposed to be like? Parents and children are going to have to learn to turn the volume down, unplug and switch off.

The slow change into adulthood is a confusing and winding path. Teenagers will travel it at different speeds and at different ages. For some, it will be smooth and easy; for most, it will be bumpy but passable; for a few, it will be painful, frightening and dangerous. The challenge for parents is to guide their teenage children through this over-stimulating, exciting and potentially frightening world.

The Teenage Process

The relationship between pre-teenage children and their parents is relatively uncomplicated. For the first few years of life children are totally dependent on their parents. They are fed, clothed, washed, hugged, loved and taught. As they get older they are able to do more for themselves but their survival and happiness are still almost completely dependent on being cared for by someone else. As children enter the teenage years they begin to become independent from their parents and they no longer need to be looked after with the same intensity. During this period they are also developing their own beliefs and values that can begin to veer away from those of their parents. This process of forging a separate identity takes a long time and teenagers test out different ideas as they grow up. Parents become the guinea pigs in this teenage identity laboratory – the safest people to test ideas on are those on whose love is guaranteed and who will stay close when things go wrong. This is one of the reasons why teenagers often behave so much worse towards their parents than to anyone else. If we behave appallingly with our friends they will dump us, but parents will almost never do this to their children, however awful they have been. This testing of values and identity can be a source of conflict between so many parents and teenagers. It can feel desperately unfair that the children we have raised, nurtured and loved seem to throw it all back in our face one day, and then the very next evening are asking to be picked up from a party because they have run out of money for a taxi.

The growth from child to adult is not linear and teenagers often lurch between these two identities. One moment they can be responsible and trustworthy and the next they are screaming and stamping their feet like a toddler. This is very confusing and undermining for parents. It's hard to know what you are going to be dealing with from one day to the next and it can cause huge frustration and anger. In my school, the children are often making fantastic progress and really beginning to change their attitude and behaviour. Then suddenly, out of the blue, something happens to them and they slide right back to almost where they started. This can be very dispiriting for the staff who have worked so hard with the children. As a school, we have become conscious of accepting the children as they are. We may not want them to take a step backwards, we may feel let down and angry because they have, but if we can't accept this reality then we can't go about helping them.

One of the most difficult challenges for parents is to adapt to whatever persona their teenager is projecting at that moment. They have to play, often in the same week, authoritative parent, nurturing parent, comforting parent, strict parent, challenging parent, friendly parent and easy-going parent, all in response to the mood of their child. It is no wonder that some just become angry parent or end up taking the path of least resistance and becoming laissez–faire parent. One day children are pushing their parents away, desperate to show that they don't need them and they are perfectly able to cope on their own, but the next they collapse because they saw their best friend flirting with a boy they fancy, and they need a cuddle. Parents can often end up with a sense of betrayal – they feel tricked into giving one response when things are going well only for it to be thrown back at them when there is a problem.

> *'Mum you let me go out on Saturday, so why aren't you letting me go out tonight?'*
>
> *'Because it's a school night.'*
>
> *'That's typical, you're always changing your mind.'*
>
> *'I am not always changing my mind, I'll have you know I …'*

I believe that there is too much pressure on young teenagers to be responsible and grown up. Parents and schools expect children to be able to conform, work independently, organise themselves, tidy up and arrive on time. Many can, but some just can't. They are still children and they need adults to continue to help them in the way they did when they were younger. I was once walking down a corridor when a teacher came out of his classroom and found his class of teenagers blocking the corridor in a large huddle. *'I can't believe it,'* he shouted. *'You're 14 years old and you still don't know how to line up properly.'*

He may have been right, perhaps at 14 they should have known how to line up, but they didn't. His frustration was caused by the gap between what he thought 14-year-olds should be able to do and what they could actually do. I felt like saying, *'It must be so frustrating when you have children who are so immature, but luckily you're a teacher, so instead of getting cross, why don't you teach them how to line up?'* Parents of teenagers will be familiar with this scenario, and the even more frustrating moments when their children suddenly seem incapable of a simple task they could have done with their eyes shut a matter of weeks before.

When teenagers are behaving like children, they need adults to treat them like children. This doesn't mean parents need to be patronising or babying, it is merely the acceptance that our children are at this in-between stage and need what they need. This means parents need to take control and be in charge, because the teenager is not in control or in charge of himself. Think of it like a boy's voice breaking. It doesn't happen in a single moment – for a long time his voice fluctuates between a man's and a child's. Sometimes, out of the blue, a word in the middle of a broken-voiced sentence comes as an embarrassing falsetto. Teenagers hover in this state between adulthood and childhood and it is the job of the parent to guide them through the process and pick up the pieces when it goes wrong. Expecting teenagers to suddenly be adults who do not need the love, the hugs, the discipline, the understanding and the patience required by younger children denies them a part of the process of growing up and creates frustration and disappointment for their parents.

This frustration can be compounded by the fact teenagers often appear to go backwards with their behaviour.

Things they could be trusted to do competently and responsibly when they were 11 suddenly become impossible for them when they hit 14. When I work with parents this is often the greatest source of their irritation. As one mother said to me, *'It is as though every inch he grows, 20 points get wiped from his IQ. If this carries on, I'm going to end up with a six-foot-two, three-year-old.'*

The Teenage Brain

What, then, is the cause of this apparent loss of intellect and responsibility? For years it was put down to the effects of an overload of hormones in the body, and certainly this is a factor. In order to kick start and maintain the process of reaching puberty, the testosterone levels of boys and the oestrogen and progesterone levels in girls begin to increase substantially. This extra dose of hormones can be a cause of mood swings, aggression and poor concentration. In addition, the introduction of sex into the teenage consciousness pushes more trivial things such as remembering to write down next week's homework aside. However, recent research suggests that the role of hormones may be overplayed in understanding changes in teenage behaviour. The focus has shifted to the development of the brain and changes that take place within its chemistry, its electrical activity and its size.

It was previously thought that the brain underwent virtually all of its development in the first few years of life and that by the time the child reached the age of seven, most of the work was done. Certainly there is a dynamic process of wiring up of the brain's neural pathways during this period, which is to a large extent controlled and affected by the experiences of nurturing and care that children receive from their parents. What has now been shown is that during the teenage years there is a second process of growth and wiring-up going on in the brain. These changes in electrical activity are now thought to be the major contributing factor in teenage behaviour. There is a shake-up of the neural pathways that connect parts of the brain and brain cells. The scrambling effect of this new growth, rewiring and reconnecting in the brain is the cause of much of the erratic, disorganised and difficult behaviour displayed by teenagers. The process is at its most intense between 13 and 17, at the time when there is the most deterioration in teenage behaviour. It continues for years afterwards and only finally settles down around the age of 28.

FOMO – The Fear Of Missing Out

When I worked in a difficult inner-city secondary school some of the behaviour was extremely challenging. Many of the teachers became very ground down by the behaviour and spent nearly all day in what I call reptile mode – the state of mind when the adrenalin levels are so high that the capacity for rational thought and action have all but gone. There was a very punitive culture and some of the staff handed out after-school detentions like Smarties.

I soon realised that rather than use the drastic sanctions that some of my colleagues were using, it was just as effective to keep the troublesome teenagers back for a couple of minutes at the end of the lesson, while the rest of the class went out on their break. This worked as well as an hour's detention, because being away from their social group as break-time commenced was a huge deterrent for teenagers. As the class left the room the children would divide up into little groups and head off in different directions. The one or two who I had kept behind would watch anxiously, as their friends disappeared on what might have been a critical moment in the structuring of friendships and teenage social grouping. Teenagers carry a dread of being away from their friends and when they are, they feel a terrible sense that they are missing out on something. The teenagers in my class rarely messed about again, so irksome was the thought of being away from their peers even for two minutes. This is a manifestation of the condition that afflicts all teenagers and we know it as FOMO – the Fear of Missing Out.

The best way for parents to understand FOMO is to think back to their own time as a teenager and remember how important social groupings and friendships were to them. As teenagers begin to loosen their ties to their parents, so they begin to ally more to their peer group and their friends within it. The approval of friends becomes at least as important as that of their parents and they can begin to follow the machinations of their peers to a slavish degree. Children begin to form more intensive friendships as they become teenagers and these, particularly with girls, can begin to resemble love affairs. The intensity of these friendships is matched by the anxiety that surrounds them. The ties and loyalty within these groups can be fickle. Teenagers will be attracted to people higher up the social pecking order whom they think are cool, attractive, sporty or merely older and they are prepared to compromise their own friendships in order to gain acceptance by the group they aspire to. FOMO becomes a sort of nagging background music throughout the teenage years. Sometimes it is loud and all pervasive, at other times, when teenagers are feeling more confident, it may quieten a little.

The Effects of FOMO

FOMO can become the biggest social driver for teenagers and explains why they appear to focus on their friendship group to the exclusion of everything else. They also become acutely sensitive to their status in the hierarchy and the most trivial interaction can take on disproportionate significance. The raised eyebrow of a friend or semi-friend will be subjected to forensic scrutiny to judge its exact meaning and what it says about their relationship. FOMO means if there is a conflict of interest between their parents' views and wishes and those of the social group, the parents will lose. Teenagers know the love of parents is resilient and deep, compared to the fast-moving soap opera that characterises their social lives. This can cause both conflict and hurt within families, as teenagers turn their backs on their parents and their values in order to stay in with their friends. The following account by Victoria, a mother I worked with, will be familiar to many parents.

The FOMO Effect: A Case Study

My daughter, Donna, spends every minute of every day thinking about her friends. Nothing else seems important to her any more. She used to spend hours playing with her hamster, now I don't think she even remembers the poor creature exists. She won't come out shopping with me any more and she never plays with her little brother. She spends her day ferociously texting her friends and starts to panic if she is more than two feet away from her phone. Her emotions are all over the shop and the other day she was in hysterics because Annie hadn't liked her new shoes. Annie has become the oracle of truth and wisdom. Anything she says goes, and my daughter hangs on every word of her woolly, ignorant pronouncements. If Annie told her it was cool to jump off a cliff she would probably do it. Meanwhile, anything I say is treated with total exasperated disdain. I seem to have lost her respect and my authority over her. Her only concern is being with her friends and if she isn't with them, she is finding out where they are and what they are up to. I have slipped down the pecking order to the level of cook, bank and washer woman. When Donna talks to her friends she is chatty, caring and funny, but she never shows that side of herself to me. When I finally met the great Annie, I was expecting a mixture of Margaret Thatcher, Mother Teresa and Angelina Jolie, so great had been the hype. In reality, she was a rather shy, perfectly polite, prettyish, teenage girl. Not, in reality, much different from my daughter. The other leader in their group is Stuart, a spotty, snotty, 15-year-old who seems to have lost the power of speech. He sits in the corner looking moody and occasionally grunting through clenched teeth while all the girls hover round him like he's James Dean. The thought that anybody could find him either interesting or attractive is beyond me. My first thought was to get him out of the front door and fumigate the house.

FOMO is one of the aspects of teenage life, like bad taste in music, which parents simply have to accept. It can often leave parents feeling rejected and hurt and the residue of these feelings can make parents resentful when their child suddenly does decide she needs them, whether for money, a lift or love. Like a three-year-old, the teenager takes what she needs from her parents and gives little in return. She is tentatively breaking away and learning both to look after herself and her friends. But because teenagers are inexperienced, and therefore not very good at looking after themselves yet, they sometimes have to go back to their parents for more support. This explains why Victoria's daughter would do anything for her friends but would do nothing for her mother. As teenage years go by and children learn to reconnect with their parents, a new, less hierarchical form of the relationship begins to develop. Many say this 'homecoming', that occurs any time from 16 well into the twenties, is one of the best things about being a parent.

Understanding Teenagers: A Summary

1. The world teenagers inhabit is more complicated and challenging than it ever was in their parents' day.
2. During the teenage years there is a growth spurt inside the brain which involves a process of rewiring of neural pathways. This change is believed to be the cause of many teenage behaviour traits.
3. Teenagers begin to develop greater loyalty to their peer group than they do to their parents, known as the FOMO effect.
4. Children can depend on the love of their parents and this is why they feel safe enough to reject them and test out what being an adult feels like.
5. The process of going from child to adult is not smooth and there are times when teenagers oscillate between the two. Parents need to recognise these facts and to try to support their children in whichever state they find them.

2

the reptile in us

Louise's Reptile Brain: A Case Study

It's half past six and Louise is coming back from a hard day's work. As she turns into her street she feels a dull ache in her stomach, which becomes more acute as she reaches her front door. She turns her key in the lock, but the door seems to be stuck. She gives it a shove and it gives way. Blocking her entrance is a pile of shoes, school bags and coats. As she picks her way past them she can feel the adrenalin starting to flow. She goes into the kitchen to be greeted by a cloud of greasy smoke and an overpowering smell of toasted cheese. On the worktop there is a carton of juice, a block of Cheddar, a loaf of bread and a slab of butter. There are crumbs everywhere and the cupboard doors and the fridge are wide open. She goes into the sitting room to find her 15-year-old son Andy lying on the sofa with his feet on the coffee table. MTV is blaring out from the television and he is talking into his mobile phone. On the floor lies the half-eaten toasted sandwich that has slipped off the plate and left a trail of crumbs all over the carpet. Louise tries to stay calm.

'Hello, darling. Please will you tidy up the kitchen?'

Andy puts his hand up to tell her to be quiet and carries on talking. Recently he has started using an accent that is part Jamaican, part New York and part South London, which Louise finds particularly irritating.

After another 30 seconds of talk to the hand, he ends the call and looks up at her.

'Andy, I could hardly get through the front door because of your mess and the kitchen is a complete state.'

'Okay, okay, give me a chance. I've just got in. I'm tired. I need to chill for a bit.'

'You can chill when you have tidied up. I don't need to come in and deal with all your mess.'

'Oh, for God's sake, why don't you just get out and leave me alone,' he shouts.

'What did I say to you only last night? What did you promise me you would do when you came in from school?' Louise replies, the tension rising in her voice.

'Why do you have to shout? Listen, I came in, the phone rang, it was John, checking what the English homework was. I talked to him. If you're so bloody desperate, why don't you clean up yourself?'

Louise now loses her temper. 'Right, that's it. If that kitchen isn't cleaned up in five minutes, then you can get out and stay out.' By now Andy has ambled over to the front door, slipped on his trainers and coat, and without a word, lets himself out. All that is left is a faint smell of tobacco in the hall.

Louise goes back into the kitchen, makes herself a cup of tea and for the second time that week, finds herself crying. Then she starts to tidy up.

Any of that sound familiar?

For many parents this is an all-too-common scenario. There is the combustible combination of a difficult, charmless teenager who won't take any responsibility for his actions and a mother who is tired and stressed after work and who is feeling she is losing authority over her son. Both of them have got stuck in a pattern of action and reaction, to the extent that conflict is becoming all they know and the defining feature of their relationship.

The Reptile Brain: Fight or Flight

Our brains evolved 50,000 years ago when we came down from the trees and became a species distinct from our primate ancestors. At the time, humans would have been nomadic hunter-gathers roaming the plains of Africa. It was a precarious existence, with potential dangers lurking behind every tree. Our bodies evolved systems to help protect us from the threat posed by wild animals. When humans are faced with a perceived danger, the body begins to prepare itself to deal with the threat. This is known as the flight-or-fight reaction. The blood vessels in the arms and legs open up and blood is diverted away from the parts of the brain that deal with rational thought to the muscles. The body is preparing to fight or run away. There is simply not enough blood to go round and, with less blood in the brain, the capacity to think clearly is reduced. The thinking part of the brain shuts down and we are left with the primeval part of our brain that is akin in complexity and understanding to that of a reptile. Under stress, our brains work with all the judgement and rationality of an alligator. This state of reduced ability to think is known as being in reptile mode.

When witnesses to a crime try to give a description of the perpetrator they are often unable to do so. During the drama of the event they go into reptile mode and the higher thinking skills that are required to remember and describe a face are lost. This also explains why witnesses to the same event can describe it in radically different ways.

The problem is that our body responds in the same way to an emotional threat as it does to a physical threat. Our physical reaction to stress hormones is the same, no matter what has caused them to be released. This means that when Louise gets home and has to deal with a slobbish, rude teenager, her body reacts as if she is being physically threatened. Louise was tired from her day at work and the levels of her stress-related hormones, adrenalin and cortisol, were already high. The feeling she had when she entered her street was a result of her body dumping another load of adrenalin into her system to cope with the trouble she was expecting when she got home. As she came through the door, she was further wound up by the coats and shoes, and then by the state of the kitchen. She did her best to contain her anger and asked Andy calmly to start tidying up, but she was already going into reptile mode. His off-hand rudeness tipped her over the edge and her attempt to have a reasonable conversation ultimately turned into a slanging match, in which both of their brains had shut down. Louise ended up making a threat to throw him out of the house that she knew wasn't realistic. When she sat down and made some tea, the blood supply to her brain began to increase again and her stress hormone levels began to reduce. As a result her anger turned to sadness. In the end she felt guilty about her reaction and the state of her relationship with Andy, so she tidied up after him to make up for it.

Think of a time when you have had a heated argument on the telephone. When you put the phone down and start to calm down, you often then think of a brilliant, cutting put-down that will have won you the argument and crushed your opponent into submission. This is an example of the reptile brain in action. During the row, your brain doesn't function and you are reduced to reptilian abuse. When you calm down, the blood supply returns and you come up with your stunning riposte, but then because you are back to being a rational, thinking human again, you realise that you have already done enough damage. The next time you pick up the phone it will probably be to apologise.

A friend of mine had recently parked outside the school gates in order to pick up his daughter. He suddenly got an enormous shunt from a car behind. Inside it were a father and his teenage son, having a blazing row. The father got out, didn't say sorry, and continued to shout at his son, blaming him for the car crash. Teenagers have a remarkable knack of sending parents into reptile mode and the outcomes can be disastrous. Our flight-or-fight reaction is very useful if we are threatened physically. Our bodies become readied for action and we can get ourselves out of trouble. The flight-or-fight reaction helps us to jump out of the way of an oncoming car or swerve to avoid a cyclist, but it is a great disadvantage when it comes to social interaction. Too much of the interaction between parents and teenagers is conducted with one or both parties in reptile mode. The result is constant conflict that exhausts everyone and leads into a spiral of mistrust, resentment and guilt that can blight the teenage years.

Wild Threats

Parents in reptile mode can get into the habit of threatening dire punishments to their teenagers in order to get them to do what they want. Louise did it with Andy when she told him he could 'get out and stay out'. At the time, it makes the parent feel strong and in control, but in reality this is a sign of weakness. Teenagers can spot a wild threat a mile away. They know that when the dust settles and everyone has calmed down, their parents are not really going to cancel their trip to France or ground them for six months. Knowing this, teenagers will often push parents even more when they make this threat, almost daring them to follow it through. This is a reactive style of parenting that will feed the bad behaviour rather than reduce it.

How Can I Stay Out of Reptile Mode?

Soldiers spend hours of their time in training taking apart their guns and putting them back together again. The process becomes second nature and they become so proficient that they can do it blindfolded.

Army training takes into account the flight-or-fight reaction and the loss of the rational brain under stress. When a gun jams on the battlefield the soldier can automatically strip the weapon down and correct the fault because he has rehearsed the procedure so many times. If he had to stop and think how to un-jam a gun while the bullets were whizzing past his ear he would not be able to do it.

Under stress, humans don't function properly. Soldiers get round this by preparing in advance. I'm not saying there is a direct comparison between looking after teenagers and going into battle, although many parents would disagree. The point is this: if parents have a clearly thought-out, well-rehearsed plan ready, when the trouble comes they will be able to stay calm, positive and keep the reptile at bay.

The Reptile in Us: A Summary

1. When humans become angry, stressed or frightened, a physical reaction means their thinking brain stops working.
2. Parents in reptile mode make wild threats that they won't follow through, which encourage the bad behaviour to happen again.
3. If parents go into reptile mode, their teenagers probably will too and things will start to get worse.
4. When parents come out of reptile mode, they often feel guilty and end up overcompensating. This teaches their children not to take them seriously when they get angry.
5. The best way to avoid going into reptile mode is to make plans and be prepared for the trouble when it comes.

3

planning for better behaviour

When parents first start following a plan, it can seem very contrived and unnatural. Some parents even say it feels manipulative, but actually it's just applying your intelligence to a problem. Once you have tried it a few times you will get used to the process and it will become second nature. You will find that making plans is effective in changing all kinds of behaviour, from day-to-day occurrences to more serious situations.

Make a Plan – Don't be a Reptile

In the last chapter we saw how parents can go into reptile mode when confronted by bad behaviour. Their response feeds into the pattern and makes the behaviour more likely to happen again. Parents get hooked into arguments with their children and end up saying and doing things they later regret. There is also the possibility that the feelings of guilt parents have after overreacting can make them over-compensate to try and make things better. Again, this response can feed the behaviour as there is a pay-off for the child. However, if parents can retrain themselves to respond in a more controlled, positive and constructive way, then they will find their teenagers' behaviour easier to manage. They will feel calmer and will not have the nagging guilt associated with parenting difficult teenagers. In this chapter I will show that preparation is the key to avoiding damaging patterns from developing and breaking away from reptile responses.

It is an uncomfortable truth for parents that the only way to change their children's behaviour is to change their own.

What Can Parents Do to Stop it Happening Next Time?

This is the challenge. What is my response to my teenager's bad behaviour and does this response make the behaviour more or less likely to happen next time? In general, parents can predict when there is going to be trouble. It may be about school and homework, it might be about staying out late or just plain rudeness. The list is endless. Despite the predictability of these situations, parents react in the same way every time. Their response feeds the behaviour and often makes it worse rather than better.

If you have found yourself trotting out expressions such as *'Every evening I have to stand over you while you do your homework'* or *'This is the third time this week you have come back late without letting me know where you were'* or *'Why are you still in bed, you are going to be late for school again!'* then it is time to take a step back and make a plan.

With some thought, it is possible to be ready for most situations. Your plan can be followed when things start to go wrong and the trouble can be short-circuited.

If you don't make a plan, the alternative is to keep on reacting to your children's behaviour in the way you always have done. This will get you more of the same behaviour.

Thinking Time

Initially parents need to think about the problem they want to address. This must be done when the teenager is not about and the parents are feeling calm. Trying to make a plan five minutes before the moment of conflict is unlikely to succeed, as the adrenalin is already flowing and the reptile brain is taking over. For the parents of many teenagers, the range and depth of behaviours they need to deal with can be overwhelming. They feel as if their child is constantly pushing boundaries, arguing and refusing to toe the line. The behaviour seems so ingrained and generalised that nothing can be done. The trick here is to break the behaviour down and to focus on one or two of the component parts. If parents are able to change things a bit, then the possibility is opened up of being able to change things a lot. Often getting a little movement gives parents a sense that things could be different and this creates a positive cycle.

It can be hard to believe at times, but the fact is that teenagers don't like the conflict either. This doesn't mean they actively avoid it as they try to set their agenda and control their lives, but in reality they want to get on with their parents.

Making a Plan

Before you discuss things with your child, sit down, pour yourself a stiff drink and ask yourself the following questions:

- *What is the behaviour I want to stop?*
  It helps to be very specific about this. If there are lots of things, start with the one you think will be the easiest to change. Once you have got into the habit of making successful plans you will find changing the more challenging behaviour easier.

- *Is it primary or secondary behaviour that is causing the biggest problem?*
  Is it the initial behaviour or the stuff that comes after it that is the biggest cause of stress?

- *When does it happen?*
  Consider who else is around at the time, as well as what time of day it happens.

- *How do I react to the behaviour?*
  It is important to be really honest here. Think about what you say and how you say it. Consider your tone

of voice and your body language. Do you come across as aggressive, plaintive, passive or assertive? And, most importantly, does your reaction make the situation better and less likely to happen again?

- *How much of the bad behaviour can I safely ignore?*
  Often simply ignoring bad behaviour will make it go away. It helps to work out what you are able to put up with.

- *What would I like to see instead?*
  Be precise and make sure you are being realistic.

- *Look at other factors that may be contributing to the problem.*
  Is my teenager getting enough sleep, is he being bullied or has he fallen out with a friend?

Planning Together

If at all possible, you should try and make the plan with your child. The more he feels part of the process the more likely it is that the plan will work. Remember that by and large teenagers do not like being in conflict with their parents and if you offer them a way for things to be better, then they will usually take it. If your teenager is really not prepared to join you in the process then you will need to impose the plan on him. This will involve a determined taking back of control that will cause considerable conflict and requires huge willpower and perseverance from the parents. You *can* make your child do something if you really want to, but it is much better if he can make himself do it. (See Chapter 8 for advice on hard cases.)

This part of the process involves sitting down with the child, talking about the behaviour and then making a plan that you can both be happy with. It is important to do this at the right time. If you try and make a plan ten minutes after you have just had a blazing row then neither of you are going to be in the right state of mind. You need to be feeling calm, otherwise the tension in your voice will immediately be picked up by your child and things will deteriorate quickly. Think carefully about where you have this talk and how you are going to initiate it. Recognise that if your child thinks she is about to be told off, then she will most likely begin to bristle. Be very clear that you are going to talk about how you are going to make things better and you are not about to give a lecture. Choose a moment when neither of you are going to be interrupted by the rest of the family or your friends. It may be useful to have some sort of peace offering, such as her favourite food, to create the right atmosphere. It may seem as if these preparations are too protracted, but the more positive you can make this conversation, the more productive the outcome is likely to be.

Once you have chosen your moment, sit down with your child and explain that the two of you seem to be arguing and fighting all the time and that you want to make a plan to help things get better. The following five steps give you a framework to guide the conversation.

1. Explain the problem to the child by simply describing what you see happening. Don't turn this into a telling-off or a lecture, or the child will start going into reptile mode and you need her to be thinking. Keep checking your voice to be sure it is calm and make sure that your body language and sitting position are not aggressive or provocative. Watch out also for the wagging finger. I emphasise these points because parents can be in such a habit of being provocative with their voices or bodies that they don't notice they are doing it. You can even give the child the job of telling you if you start wagging your finger or sounding cross – using a bit of self-deprecation and humour at these moments can be a good way to keep her on your side. It helps if you take some of the blame yourself, however much you feel it isn't your fault. Remember, you are trying to reach a solution here, you are not holding a trial.

   'I feel every time I ask you to do something you turn round and snap at me. Usually this happens when I ask you something quite reasonable, such as whether you have practised your piano. This makes me cross and we usually have a row which leaves us both feeling fed up.'

2. Give her the right to reply and engage her thinking brain.

   'You must be really fed up with me nagging, just as I'm really fed up with you snapping at me. What can

we do to make things easier so I don't nag and you don't snap?'

She may then simply shrug and say, *'I dunno.'* Don't be wound up by this. It is often a defence mechanism to play for time.

3. Offer a solution.
'How about we say I will ask you in as nice a voice as possible to practise? I won't then stand over you, but I will expect you to start within five minutes of being asked.'

4. Offer a reward.
'If you manage to practise your piano within five minutes of me asking five nights in a row then I will cook your favourite lunch on Sunday.' (See Chapter 6: Rewarding your Teenager.)

5. Have a consequence ready.
'If you ignore me, then I will take 50 pence off your pocket money.' (See Chapter 7: Punishments and Consequences.)

The important thing is to keep the conversation positive and solution-focused. You don't want to end up having a row and you want the child to feel she has been listened to. When you have finished the conversation you can thank and praise her for listening to you.

Making the Plan Work

- It is important to be positive and expect it to be a success. Remind the child in advance what the agreement is before you give out the instruction. It will help to engage her brain if you give her a bit of lead-up time.

  'I am going to ask you to practise your piano in a moment, remember our deal.'

- When you ask her to practise, as soon as she starts, give her some subtle praise. Don't go over the top with hyperbole, just give a little recognition for following the instruction.

  'Oh, thanks for doing that.'

- Repeat the process next time, focusing on the previous success.

  'You practised so well yesterday, can you do it again now please?'

  By referring back, you are staying positive and giving her a little praise to encourage her.

- Stick with it. At some stage she is bound to test you out to see if you mean business. If you negotiated a consequence for not practising, or tidying up or snapping, then you must follow through with it. Do this calmly and don't get hooked in by any secondary behaviour.

  'You didn't tidy up within the five minutes, so you lose 50 pence, according to our agreement.'

By referring back to the agreement you are stopping things becoming personal. The message is, '*It's not me being horrible, it's the deal that we both signed up to.*' Don't, whatever you do, be tempted to use the reward or the consequence for any other behaviour. This immediately devalues it. Remember to keep praising.

Julia's Homework Trouble with Marcus: A Case Study

Julia kept getting complaints from school about her 14 -year-old son Marcus. She had notes home from his maths and English teachers about his failure to complete homework on time and his head of year has been on the phone about his general attitude to school. When Julia confronted him about the work he said it wasn't a big deal, he did the work, he just gave it in a day or two late, and anyway, the maths teacher didn't like him.

Julia started trying to check up on his homework by asking to see his school journal, but there was nothing in it because the teachers email the homework to the children. She started asking him about homework as soon as he got in from school. Then one afternoon he came in, slumped down in front of the television and refused to talk. Julia saw red and went over and switched the television off.

'I want to see your homework now!' she shouted.

This set him off and he began to shout back, saying it was none of her business and that the thing that stopped him doing the work was the fact that she nagged him all the time.

'You never let me do anything I want,' he screamed. 'you treat me like a baby, I'm not six you know!'

'Well, you act like a bloody six-year-old. Look at you, slobbing round the house, I have to clear up after you, you don't change your clothes unless I tell you to, you have the table manners of a pig and...'

By then he had got up from the sofa and marched up to his bedroom and the last part of Julia's rant was to an empty room. For a few days afterwards, she backed off, not wanting to make the situation worse and assuming she had got the message across about completing homework. You can imagine her and fury when she got another phone call from his maths teacher saying he hadn't produced any homework for two weeks.

She went up to his room to confront him, but he burst into tears and said the work was too difficult and he couldn't do it. Julia ended up crying too, apologising for being such a nag and telling him how clever he was. She came down from his room feeling really guilty, but also cross because his tears had stopped her from confronting the issue. She knew that Marcus was a bright boy who could easily do the homework, but was getting so far behind that he didn't know what he was supposed to be doing.

This scenario is not uncommon. For some reason or another, a bright teenager gets turned off schoolwork. There can be many different roots to the problem – for example, a personality clash with a teacher or a loss of affection for the subject. Often, however, it is because a lot of new distractions have arrived, which seem much more important than school, such as girls, parties and changes within friendship groups. It is an unfortunate reality that at exactly the same time as they are doing some of the most important exams of their life, teenagers are also overloaded with all these other excitements.

Here is a plan that helped Julia get Marcus back on track.

1. *Sit down and discuss the problem*

   Julia chose a time when Marcus was calm and outlined the issue to him. She explained that because he wasn't doing his homework he was falling behind and that both she and the teachers were worried that this could affect his exam grades. Julia tried to keep her own frustration and anger out of the conversation because she didn't want Marcus to feel attacked. If she allowed this to happen then he would go into reptile mode and the conversation would turn into a row.

2. *Ask for his views*

   When she did this, Marcus said if everyone just left him alone then he would do the work. It was the hassle that was stopping him from getting anything done. Julia knew Marcus wasn't being realistic and so she was going to need to impose a solution on him for the time being. There are times when teenagers aren't able to be mature and grown up about what is going on. When they revert to this childish state, the adults will need to take control until things have improved. Put simply, when the teenager is behaving like a child, then he will need a solution for a child. Parents have to accept that at times, teenagers will revert to being childish. There is nothing wrong with this, it is all part of growing up.

3. *Talk to the school*
Julia went into the school and talked face-to-face with Marcus's teachers. This is a far more effective way of getting to the root of the problem and finding a solution than using the telephone or email. Teachers appreciate parents who come in and show that they are taking the school's concerns seriously. As the homework was all emailed, Julia asked to be copied into all correspondence, so she knew what needed to be done and what the deadlines were. She also agreed to meet with the teachers again in a month's time, to monitor progress.

4. *Make a set time for homework*
Julia stipulated that Marcus was going to do his homework when he got in at around 4.30pm every evening. Julia was lucky because she got back from work at about the same time as her son. When the homework was finished, Julia would check it before Marcus could go and do his own thing.

5. *Reduce the distractions*

Marcus was going to have to work at his mother's desk in her bedroom where there would be none of the distractions found in his room. He would also have to give her his phone until the work was complete. Marcus made a real fuss about this.

'I need my phone to talk about the work with my friends,' he pleaded.

'If you need to call anyone, then ask me and you can use your phone,' she answered.

6. *Set a time limit*

Julia told Marcus that the plan would continue for a month. If Marcus could stick to it then he could go back to a more relaxed regime, with the proviso that if he let things slip then he would have to go back to the plan.

7. *Don't give up*

Julia was prepared for Marcus to make a real fuss for the first week or so to see if she was serious about the plan. She also expected him to try and broker deals, such as *'Okay, I'll do half now and then finish the rest later.'*

She had to resist all of these pleas, however charming and sweet he was being, as to give in once would effectively put the whole plan up for negotiation.

8. *Praise him*

Julia was ready to praise Marcus whenever he followed the plan. Praise him for giving up his phone, praise him for settling down to the work, praise him for finishing the work. Julia also brought him up a sandwich and a drink once he had got going as a reward, as well as a way of checking he was getting on with it.

9. *Ignore the grumbling*
As much as possible, the plan was for Julia to ignore any low-level sulking and avoid getting hooked into an argument. Moaning and grumbling are often used by teenagers as a way of sidetracking the adult away from the main issue.

10. *Offer a reward*
Julia knew that at first Marcus was going to really struggle with motivation, so in order to get him kick-started she offered him a five-pound iTunes voucher every Sunday if all the homework was completed.

11. *And a consequence*
Julia wasn't messing about. If the work wasn't done, then Marcus couldn't go out on either Friday or Saturday night.

The plan Julia set up for Marcus was very tight and well worked out. She was being firm with him, as she had decided that was what he needed at the time. She knew that homework was going to play a significant part in his life for the next few years and she wanted to get it sorted before it became a perennial problem. Marcus did make a big fuss at first, as Julia had predicted, and he wasn't allowed out during the first weekend. By the middle of the second week he was handing over his phone without much grumbling and he finished his homework. That weekend he went out in the evenings and got his iTunes voucher on Sunday. The next two weeks went really well, with Marcus getting straight down to work when he got home from school. The review with the school was a positive meeting. Marcus's teachers had noticed a genuine improvement both in his work and his attitude to school.

At the end of the month, Julia congratulated Marcus for doing so well and she told him that he was free to do his homework when he wanted to for the time being. Interestingly, Marcus chose to continue to do his homework at his mother's desk as soon as he got back from school. Like most teenagers, he secretly liked the routine and he had learnt to get away from that horrible, dull ache that was caused by having homework hang over him. Getting his work done made Marcus feel generally better about being in school and this was the cause of the improved attitude his teachers had noticed.

Planning for Better Behaviour: A Summary

1. Planning allows parents to respond calmly and predictably to conflict moments. The reptile is kept at bay.
2. Planning should be done when you are relaxed. Try to include your teenager in the process.
3. Plans must be realistic. Don't make a plan you won't be able to stick to. Try to focus on one bit of behaviour you want to change.
4. Keep trying. If you give up and go back to the old pattern the child won't take you seriously next time you try and change things.
5. Notice when things have improved and let the child know you have noticed.
6. Praise more often than you used to criticise.

4

communicating with teenagers

'Hello, Jake, how are you?'

'Okay.'

'How was your day at school?'

'Okay.'

'Have you got much homework?'

'Yup.'

'What is it?'

'Oh, stuff.'

'Darling, is everything okay? You're very quiet.'

'Yup.'

Parent reptile brain engaged.

'Can you at least look at me when I'm talking to you? I'm asking if you're okay.'

Teenage reptile brain engaged.

'I just told you I'm fine. Stop going on at me.'

'I don't think checking you're okay is going on at you. I am your mother, you know.'

'Okay, okay, I'm fine, I'm okay, everything's okay, please can you give me some peace?'
'How dare you ...'

For many parents an invisible barrier seems to sit between them and their teenage children that prevents any meaningful communication, allowing only nagging, moaning and requests for food, transportation and money.

'I hear her on the phone to her friends and she doesn't stop talking and laughing, but she can hardly bring herself to look at me, let alone say anything. I would love to be able to have a conversation with her like we used to. When she was 11 we used to have a real laugh together.'

It can be heart-breaking for parents to suffer this rejection when their child appears to turn his back on their love. Part of the process of being a teenager is learning to live independently without needing to be looked after by parents. Teenagers spend a lot of time unconsciously testing out this new and scary independence in the knowledge that if it doesn't quite work out then they can go scurrying back to the safety of their parents. They are experimenting with being grown up at the same time as feeling like children. Parents are on the receiving end of this social game because they are the safest people to experiment on. Children don't feel certain of much when they are teenagers, but one thing they can usually rely on is the unconditional love of their parents. They can ignore them, reject them, argue with them, fight with them and exasperate them and still be loved and accepted. Although at times this love can be stretched to the limit and parents can feel like chucking their monstrous teenager out, in reality, no matter how appallingly their child behaves, they very rarely do. Instead, parents often labour through their children's teenage years in semi-reptile mode, waiting for the storm to blow over and looking forward to easier times somewhere in the future.

Better Communication with Teenagers

It can be hard for parents to accept that they have to be the starting point for any improvements in communication. The child's behaviour is unlikely to improve unless the parent is prepared to change the way they do things. It is easy for parents to become stuck with the view that it is the child who is causing the trouble and therefore him that needs to change. There is often so much anger around a challenging teenager that the necessary calm reflection is difficult to achieve. A useful mindset is to think in terms of changing the pattern of behaviour that has developed, rather than focusing too much on the people involved. Break down the pattern and the people will change with it.

Tone, Timing and Text

Having spent many years observing adults and teenagers interact through my work, I have developed the three Ts, which are the fundamentals of good communication. The three Ts are tone, timing and text. The tone is how you say it, the timing is when you say it and the text is what you say.

Let's look back at the conversation at the beginning of the chapter. It started with Tom's mother coming in and asking him how he was, a perfectly reasonable question. He grunted an answer and then went back to whatever he was doing. His mother decided to push him a bit and use a new text, but she couldn't get him to respond so she started to ask him if there was something wrong. The subtext was '*It is only acceptable to be this rude and monosyllabic if you are feeling upset about something. Therefore there must be something wrong, otherwise I am justified in being annoyed by your attitude.*' His offhand reply put her into reptile mode, but she was on her way there a long time before that. This gave Tom his get out as well, because instead of having to have a discussion about his homework or how he was feeling, he could get away from the spotlight by having a row. Asking how a teenager is and asking him how much homework he has got are both perfectly reasonable questions. It was because they were asked at the same time, that Tom was on his guard. It may have been that Tom's initial reluctance to get involved in the conversation was because he knew where it was going to end up. If Tom's mother had simply said *'Hello'* and checked how he was without mentioning homework then the conversation might have been easier. The trickier subject of homework could have been raised later, but at least the two of them would have had one reasonable conversation in the bank before homework was even mentioned. It may be that Tom will need to be picked up on how he welcomes his mother, but if he doesn't think saying *'Hello'* is the precursor to a conversation about homework, then he might be more friendly in the first place.

> *'Tom, if I come in and say "Hello", please will you look at me and say 'Hello" back? I promise I won't talk about anything like homework when I first come through the door.'*

This change in the timing, tone and text of the conversation will make for a more harmonious return from work and school, at a time when we are all tired and can easily slip into reptile mode. Let's look at this in a bit more detail.

Tone

If parents and teenagers were able to listen to recordings of themselves they would hear the tone in which so many conversations are carried out. If you didn't speak a word of English and you listened in, you would quickly be able to work out the emotional state of the speakers and the irritation in their voices. The tone parents and teenagers use with each other can develop into a pattern, which means that every conversation carries some of the anger and frustration that both parties are feeling. Parents are so certain that the response from their teenager will be stroppy when they ask them, for example, to tidy their room, that there is a tendency to get the retaliation in first and go in fighting. Similarly, teenagers become so used to hearing the hectoring tone of their parents that they respond to it whether it has really been used or not.

Tone of voice is like a delivery system for the message. It helps to convey meaning, it shows how the speaker is feeling and it sets up the course of the conversation. We are all extremely responsive to the tone people use with us. Think about what an important factor good service is in our enjoyment of a meal, or how the best food in the world can be ruined by an offhand, unfriendly waiter.

If parents are able to become mindful of their tone and notice when it sounds aggressive or irritable, then that is one of the first steps to improving communication with teenagers. The human sensitivity to tone also makes us react to our teenagers, so that we can quickly become annoyed by how they say things. Again, mindfulness is the key to not getting hooked in to an argument. If, as parents, we can learn to contain our irritation rather than be drawn in, then we can begin to break the pattern. I am not for a minute underestimating how hard this can be – I recognise that the tone of so much of teenagers' communication is designed to get right under their parents' skin. I was recently working with a mother who was particularly exasperated by her teenage son. As an experiment, I measured her pulse and then asked her to imagine her son for a few minutes. When I took her pulse again, it had gone up from 80 to 100. I think this would be typical for a lot of parents.

Timing

Some conversations are difficult to have and it is hard to find the right time to embark on one. '*The school has been in touch and you haven't been doing your homework*' or '*Whenever I ask you to do anything you fly into a rage and storm off*' are never going to be easy conversation openers. However, there are, without doubt, wrong moments to have these conversations if we want to achieve a positive outcome and maintain a good relationship. The parent who decides to tell her teenager off in front of her friends is asking for trouble. The love of a mother is guaranteed, but the acceptance by a group of friends by a FOMO-obsessed teenager feels precarious, so being offhand or rude to her mother is a much safer option than being meek and uncool. As we saw in the example between Tom and his mother, that interface moment, when the teen has got back from school and is tired and grumpy and a parent has got back from work and is equally tired and grumpy, is another hopeless time to try and have a remotely difficult conversation. As a rule of thumb, the trickier the text of the conversation, the more parents need to think about the timing.

There are some teenagers for whom it is never a good time. They are spring-loaded to fly off the handle when anything is mentioned that might suggest that they have done something wrong or there is something that they need to do. This is as much a behaviour issue as a communication issue and can be dealt with using behaviour techniques or praise, rewards and sanctions which I will discuss in later chapters. However, if parents are able to improve their tone and text then they may find their child becomes more responsive more often and so getting the timing right will become easier.

Text

Think of any difficult conversation that you need to have with a spouse, a friend or a work colleague. Often we plan in advance what we are going to say, the words we are going to use and how we want things to turn out. When people have a difficult phone call to make, it's quite common to write a little script for themselves to ensure they say what they mean to say. This preparation means that in the heat of the moment, when the adrenalin starts to flow and we go into reptile mode, we manage to get our message across without getting caught up by either our own or the other person's emotions. With younger children, parents are usually able to get away with being more direct with instructions. *'Okay, you two, get dressed now, thanks'* would work well with a couple of eight-year-olds. But if we spoke like that to a teenager it might well be the precursor to a row. This is not that surprising. If we spoke to a colleague at work or to a spouse with the same brusque words we use with young children, we would cause offence.

While I am working with teenagers they frequently complain that they are expected to behave like adults, while being talked to like children. It is easy for parents to slip into brusque mode, but the inevitable outcome is that the teenager slips into sulky child mode. Remember that with teenagers what you dish out, you will probably get back.

When I worked in a secondary school, I would track behaviour in different classes. One of the teachers particularly disliked a class I was working with. She would sit in the staffroom and moan that they were rude, lazy and childish. These three adjectives could have been applied perfectly to that teacher. Her lessons were disorganised and underprepared; she had never learnt the children's names; she barked orders at them and she would get into petty arguments. On one occasion such an argument ended with her sitting at the front of the class with her arms folded saying, *'Right! That's it! I'm not going to talk to this class for five minutes!'* She blamed the children for everything, but she couldn't see that she was reaping what she was sowing. A different teacher, further along the corridor, gave the impression that it was a rare privilege for her to teach this class and she was friendly, calm and authoritative. The children loved her and behaved brilliantly.

Before starting a difficult conversation with a teenager it really helps for parents to do a quick audit of their own emotional state. If you can feel yourself bristling then, if possible, take a minute or two to calm down before you start talking. Consider what outcome you want from the conversation before you start. All too often parents start to moan at their teenager without any focus on a solution, the result is usually a row. Get the first few words of the conversation right, show a bit of empathy and you are more likely to get the outcome you want:

> *'Kelly, it's probably the last thing you feel like doing, but we need to talk about the way you are speaking to me. I feel every time I ask you to do anything I get sulks or abuse. You wish you didn't have to do homework, I wish you didn't have to do homework, but it has to be done and if you don't get down to it then it is my job to hassle you about it. I hate doing it, believe me, but I would also hate to see you underachieve in school. Have I got a point? What do you think?'*

Parents who have learnt to take the three Ts of communication into account when talking to teens will not always get charming and compliant responses. Teenagers can easily slip back into child mode and become rude and petulant. When this happens it is all too easy for parents to be sucked in by this behaviour and turn into children themselves. If parents are alert and aware of their own behaviour and responses, they can avoid getting hooked in and ultimately find that moments of conflict become less frequent. It is as much a challenge for parents to get used to communicating with their children as grown-ups as it is for teenagers to grow into behaving like adults.

Communication Problems: A Case Study

Barbara had become increasingly worried about her relationship with her 15-year-old daughter, Jo. In the last year she had begun to feel more and more shut out of Jo's life. Jo was very sociable and would spend every possible minute in some form of electronic communication with her friends. At school she was doing okay, but Barbara got the feeling that Jo, who was a bright girl, was coasting. Jo became very wary about any sort of communication with her mother and soon the only conversations she would become involved in were glib arrangements about being picked up or dropped off or about what food she wanted. Jo had become noticeably moodier lately and she would argue and storm off if she was asked to do anything she didn't want to do. Barbara found herself getting more and more impatient with Jo and even the sight of her scruffy, graffitied school bag in the hall started to irritate her. Every conversation was conducted in surly sarcasm and the two of them could hardly bear to be in the same room together. Barbara put most of this down to typical teenager behaviour, but then a couple of times she caught Jo crying. She repeatedly asked what was wrong, but Jo brushed her aside and simply said, 'Nothing, everything's fine.'

Barbara asked me to get involved and I said I would as long as Jo was also prepared to be part of the process. With a child as old and as clearly intelligent as Jo, I was convinced that getting her cooperation was going to be the most effective way forward. A week later Barbara called back and said they were both prepared to give it a go. For the first session I got them together in the same room, but they were almost incapable of saying anything civil to each other and the first half hour was very tense. I introduced the rule that no one was allowed to discount a compliment and then I asked them to think of one nice thing to say about the other one. This may have seemed superficial, but I wanted to get a sense of how bad things were. Jo was quickly able to say she liked her mother's cooking. I asked her what her particular favourite was and she said soup. I asked what sort and Jo said carrot and orange. I reminded Barbara about accepting compliments, but she found it very hard to take this positive comment from her daughter. I had to stop her from qualifying her thanks by making a barbed remark about how often Jo actually turned up for tea.

When it came to her turn, Barbara sat in silence for a long time, and then began to cry. Then Jo began to cry too. Barbara was so stuck in a negative rut that she couldn't find a single positive thing to say about her daughter. After a few minutes she was able to tell Jo she had a lovely singing voice. Jo seemed genuinely touched.

Next we began to discuss some of the issues that they wanted to work on, but I kept the session quite short because I could easily see it turning into a slanging match. I left them with some homework, which was to think of another positive thing to say about each other at the next meeting and also to imagine what they would see and hear if communication improved between them.

The next week was much easier. With more time they had both thought of compliments they could pay each other. They agreed that over the week they would give each other three compliments or little bits of praise. I didn't want anything too grandiose, because everything had to be genuine. I didn't want them to make up nice things to please me, as it would make the whole process artificial.

Next we discussed the things they would most like to change. They both came out with the same thing, but from their own different angle.

Barbara said, 'When I ask you to do something, I would love you to do it without arguing or throwing a strop.'

Jo said, 'I would like you to ask me to do things rather than just to tell me what to do. I would like you to give me some time to do it and not to start shouting or going on at me if I don't do it straight away.'

'Okay,' said Barbara, 'I will ask you nicely, but when I do, please don't have a strop at me and if I am going to try not to stand over you, then I need to be able to trust you to do whatever it is in a reasonable amount of time.'

'All right, I won't strop if you ask me nicely and I will get things done.'

'Shake on it,' I said, but instead they gave each other a hug and the tears started again.

We met again after a month and the change was obvious. The two of them sat close to each other on the sofa. When I first met them they sat in separate chairs.

I asked them how the giving and receiving of instructions had gone. They both agreed things were much better. They had both made a conscious effort to follow the plan and they had been good at reminding each other to stick to it. They were still managing to find things to praise about each other. They had had some spectacular rows over the month and things were by no means perfect. This was to be expected, I said, but the most important thing was that the lines of communication were now open between them again and they had remembered how much they loved each other.

The 10 Rules of Communication with Teenagers

1. *Tone*

Always be aware of the way in which you speak to your teenager. Try to hear your voice and how the tone you use conveys meaning and emotion. When you are raising difficult issues try to keep your tone neutral and matter-of-fact. The more mindful you are of the tone you use, the better communication will be.

2. *Timing*

Avoid having tricky conversations at the naturally reptilian moments of the day, such as first thing in the morning, when you have just got back from work or on a Sunday evening. The chance of having harmonious communication at these times is low.

3. *Text*

When you have something difficult to say to your teenager, prepare a script in advance. Try and work out what you want to say and how you are going to say it. A few minutes of preparation will help you to stay out of reptile mode and enable you to keep your emotions under control. Work out when you are going to embark on the conversation and what your opening few lines are going to be.

4. *Empathy*

Acknowledge your teenager's feelings and frustration. A little bit of empathy will help to get him on side.

'I know you're not going to like this, but I need your room tidied this evening because the plumber is coming tomorrow and he needs to get to your radiator.'

'You must get so fed up at times, coming back from a hard day at school and then having to do all this homework.'

'I know it's really annoying that I have different rules about when you have to be back in the evening compared to some of your friends.'

5. *Use fantasy to make reality bearable*

How about trying a few of these:

One day robots will do all the cleaning, until then its up to us.

'Imagine if they did some research that concluded that all homework was a waste of time and you never had to do it again?'

'It would be great if the world became so safe that teenagers could go out as late as they wanted without their parents needing to worry.'

'I wish I could make school begin at 11 o'clock for you.'

6. *Use humour*

Teenagers can at times seem to have a total sense of humour failure when it comes to their parents, so your need to tread carefully. Avoid sarcasm or anything that sounds like a put-down. Teenagers are far less confident and more sensitive than they seem. However, a little gentle ribbing helps to keep the relationship good, even if the biggest laugh you can get out of your teenager is a dry *'Ha, ha.'*

7. *Apologise*

When you get things wrong, put your hands up and say sorry. This can be very difficult to do if a teenager is constantly criticising or annoying you, but by apologising, you are modelling how to be a functioning adult and owning up to your own human failings.

8. *Use alternatives to talking*

The very process of starting a conversation with a teenager can be the cause of trouble. If the teenager responds rudely or aggressively to your opener, it is hard not to get hooked into a row. Sending texts or leaving a well-placed note can get the message across without setting up a confrontation. Adding some praise or acknowledging feelings can help to sugar the pill.

Please would you take the washing out of the machine and hang it up? Otherwise it is going to smell. (I know you did this last week as well, thanks for being so helpful.)

Thanks.

Annoying request! When you get in please could clean the sink in the bathroom?

Thanks.

9. *Praise*

Don't forget to give lots of well-timed descriptive praise when your teenager is communicating well. (See Chapter 5: The 6 to 1 Strategy.)

10. *Start by saying something nice*

When you get back in the evening, start by saying something nice to your teenager without tempering it with an instruction or a criticism.

'Good evening, lovely to see you.'

'Oh good, you're back, I want to ask your advice about something.'

'I've missed you.'

This mustn't be artificial. It's much better to say something small and genuine than coming out with hyperbole.

Getting Teenagers to Talk

One of the biggest concerns for parents is the way in which they can feel shut out of their teenager's life. They can deal with the fact that their children talk more to their friends than to them, but when their children are obviously unhappy or distressed and they won't talk, then parents start to really worry. Parents try to encourage their children to be open, but often the more they push the more the teenager clams up.

Why Won't They Talk?

There is no doubt that most teenagers would like to talk to their parents when they have a problem. They don't do it because they are worried about the reaction they will receive. If they have done something wrong, they might be told off. If they have done something stupid, they might be ridiculed. If they have done something dangerous, their parents will be shocked. In order to feel safe enough to talk, teenagers have to feel that they aren't going to be judged or belittled. This throws up a real tension for parents, perfectly described by this father who was having a difficult time with his 16-year-old daughter.

'If my child tells me something terrible that she has done then surely I need to show that I don't approve, otherwise I am neglecting my duty as a good parent? I can't pretend I don't mind when I do. We are talking about honesty here. I can't lie to my children in order to get them to confess to me.'

Don't Push Them

When teenagers seem upset there is a temptation to come out bluntly and ask what the problem is.

'You've been sulking round the house all day, is something the matter?'

'Is something bothering you? It's not like you to be upset.'

The most likely answer to either of these questions is *'No, I'm fine.'* The veiled criticism and the mild annoyance of the parent will have been picked up by the teenager and there is little chance of him feeling like talking.

Name It

When a teenager is sulking or seems to be upset, it can be useful for parents to simply say what they see.

'You seem upset today.'

These statements open the door to talk if the teenager wants to, without hassling him.

It can also be useful to name what you think the problem is. If the parent guesses right the child may well respond, if not there is no harm done.

'Are you annoyed because I wouldn't let you go out tomorrow night?'

'You seem upset. Has something been going on at school?'

'Emma hasn't been around for a bit and you seem upset. Have the two of you had some sort of row?'

Parents should avoid being pushy or starting a game of twenty questions, but they shouldn't be afraid to ask.

Another way of showing empathy and understanding is to notice and name the predominate emotion your child is feeling. So if she says, *'I have worked on my project all weekend and I now I think I have accidentally wiped it from my computer,'* try saying, *'How frustrating, you must be fuming.'* Much more useful than the tempting, *'How many times have I told you to back up work? I have no sympathy.'*

Don't Offer Solutions

When teenagers start to talk about something that is worrying them, parents often feel they need to offer a solution.

'A group of girls in my class are stopping me from joining in their conversations. I'm sure they're saying things about me.'

'Well, why don't you go into school tomorrow and have a word with them?If that doesn't work, then tell the teacher.'

It is far more effective to let teenagers work out their own solution, than to tell them what to do. They are often not talking to their parents because they want advice, but simply because they want to be listened to. You don't have to say anything.

Sometimes nodding to show you are listening and making some affirming noises like *'Okay'* or *'I see'* or *'Uh huh'* is enough to let a teenager know he is being heard.

Try Not to Make Judgements

If teenagers think you are judging what they are saying then they will almost certainly stop talking. Try not to make a judgement and simply listen; you can have your say later if you need to. Usually you won't have to say you disapprove, your child will already have a pretty good idea of where your moral standpoint is likely to be.

'Two girls in my class are taking drugs.'

'That's terrible, give me their names and I will get in touch with the head teacher. It's disgraceful that this sort of thing should be going on in school.'

This is guaranteed to make the child regret what she has said. A less judgemental and more dispassionate answer would be much better here.

'Really? How did you find out?'

Later on it is fine to state or restate your own moral view on the subject and to emphasise why you have taken that position.

'It worries me when teenagers are taking drugs because their brains are still growing and they could be doing themselves real harm. Also, they are breaking the law and could get into a whole lot of trouble with the police.'

Offer Your Child a Chance to Talk

Without being pushy or putting your teenager on the spot, it is helpful to show you are available to listen.

'You seem pretty fed up, would it help to talk about it?'

'I'm here to listen if there's something you want to talk about.'

Getting children to talk comes down to the three Ts of communication: Tone, Timing and Text. If teenagers feel they can talk to their parents without ending up on the receiving end of a lecture, then they will gain the confidence to be more open and better able to talk through things that are worrying them.

Communicating with Teenagers: A Summary

1. Part of the separation process for teenagers involves communicating more with friends and interacting less with parents. This can be hurtful for parents.

2. Remember the three Ts of communication: Tone – how you say it, Timing – when you say it, and Text – what you say. Get these right and teenagers will communicate better.

3. Be mindful of how irritating it can be communicating with a teenager and try not to get hooked in by rude or aggressive behaviour. If you go into reptile mode, you can be fairly certain they will too.

4. If you want teenagers to talk, try to be open, empathetic, calm and non-judgemental. If you need to show your disapproval wait until they have had their say and then explain why you think the behaviour is wrong, bearing in mind that they probably know what your views are already.

section two

how to get better behaviour

5

the 6 to 1 strategy

I spent three years working with disaffected 14-year-old boys. These boys were in danger of permanent exclusion from school and were beginning to get acquainted with the criminal justice system. We set them individual behaviour targets and allowed them to choose their own reward from a list they had drawn up. The rewards they chose ranged from a trip to the cinema, to extra football, to lunch at McDonald's. When they had achieved their target and I asked them what reward they would like from the list they almost universally said, '*Just tell my mum I've been good.*'

These were boys who were in almost permanent conflict with their parents and yet they were still desperate to receive praise from them. We humans have a desire for recognition from our parents that never leaves us. Even grown adults whose parents have died years before continue to do things simply because their mother or father would approve.

This chapter will show that using praise is the most effective tool parents have for getting better behaviour from their children and raising their self-esteem. The more praise given out, the better the behaviour will become. Parents who give out the most praise have better behaved children than those who are constantly looking to criticise and correct bad behaviour. It seems like an enormous contradiction, but the worse the behaviour, the more praise is required. Ultimately, if parents are able to average six pieces of praise for every one bit of criticism or telling off, they will quickly notice a change not only in their children, but also in themselves. I call this my 6 to 1 strategy.

As children reach adolescence, approval from their friends appears to become more important than approval from their parents. Nevertheless, positive feedback and support from parents remains as essential for supporting teenagers as it is for potty-training a three-year old.

In my work supporting teachers I have spent many hours observing in classrooms. I used this simple tally to keep a record of praise and criticism in the classroom:

Positive comments	Negative comments
✔ ✔ ✔ ✔ ✔	✔ ✔

Some teachers seemed to give out praise constantly, while others could only nag. One sorry teacher gave out 47 pieces of criticism without once praising anyone in a half-hour lesson. Sadly, this was not untypical. What I quickly noticed was that the teachers who praised the most had the best-behaved classes. When teachers got the ratio of praise to criticism up to around 6 to 1, incidents of bad behaviour all but disappeared.

At first, I thought this was simply because these teachers had easier classes, but then, I tracked classes as they went from teacher to teacher throughout the day. Quite simply, the higher the praise-to-criticism ratio, the better the behaviour. Where the teacher was positive, the children came into the classroom ready to learn and expecting to enjoy the lesson. I then began tape-recording teachers and getting them to tally their own praise-to-criticism ratios, setting them the target of getting up to 6 to 1. Those who managed to achieve it (and not everyone could, old habits die hard) saw a remarkable improvement in the behaviour of the children in their classes. Outside the classroom in my work with parents, using the 6 to 1 strategy has the same dramatic effect. When parents are able to radically increase the amount of praise they give out, there will be a significant improvement in their children's behaviour. When they get up to 6 to 1 with their children, the bad behaviour all but disappears.

It is easy to praise when the behaviour is good, but when the behaviour gets worse, keeping the 6 to 1 ratio up is really hard. It goes right against the grain to praise a teenager who seems hell-bent on annoying you.

When the way for children to get noticed by their parents is by doing the right thing, then their behaviour will begin to improve. When the behaviour has become really challenging, parents have to make a conscious effort to notice and praise things the child is doing right. After all, if your 14-year-old is winding up his little sister every five minutes, then there are four minutes and 59 seconds when he is not winding her up and can be praised. Parents can easily get out of the habit of praising and forget the power of catching their children being good.

If parents are prepared to try it, they will find that this simple 6 to 1 strategy works for changing any sort of behaviour.

Using 6 to 1

6 to 1 is counter-intuitive. It takes practice and real commitment on the part of the parents. Catching teenagers being good helps to change the currency of recognition in the home from negative to positive and *will* change their behaviour. Initially, parents need to understand that if their child is not misbehaving, then there will be something to praise. This focus on the positive will usually begin to take effect in a few days, though it may take slightly longer for teenagers whose behaviour is more serious. Remember, thanks to the reptile brain, it is

impossible to start this new regime when you are in the middle of a battle. People who are stressed are not in a position to take on change.

Teenagers need to be praised in a more subtle way than younger children. You can't get away with the burlesque, pantomime performance that is so effective with the under-fives. The timing is also important. If you praise your teenage son for finishing his homework when he is standing with a group of his cool friends, you are likely to get the compliment thrown back in your face. When you get the timing right you will be amazed how he laps up the praise and how effective it is in getting him to behave. Teenagers won't always be as overtly responsive to praise as younger children, they may appear to take little notice, but they will be absorbing it. This chapter shows parents how to use praise effectively to change and improve behaviour.

It is easy for our focus to become too narrow with teenage children. We can get so caught up with our irritation about their annoying qualities that we forget how good they are in so many other respects. By reducing the criticism and increasing the amount of praise, it becomes possible to change the emphasis of the relationship. Very often, changing teenage behaviour can be a case of reducing the attention given to their faults and spotting and praising their good qualities. Teenage children can be irritating in so many ways and parents can easily get caught into a negative cycle of moaning and nagging. Teenagers won't change their behaviour unless parents change theirs.

How to Use the 6 to 1 Strategy

When I first started teaching I had a fantastic boss. At the end of every term he would write a postcard to each member of staff with a short personal note listing one or two successes he had noticed and thanking them for all their hard work. As we got to the end of each term I used to look forward to his card and when it arrived I would keep it and sometimes refer back to it when I had had a particularly awful day. I wish I'd told him how much I appreciated those cards. I never had the nerve to go into his office and thank him. But during my first few years teaching, when my confidence was at its lowest and I had days when I felt completely out of my depth, knowing I had a boss who supported and cared for me helped me to keep going. I loved receiving the praise, but I never showed it. Praising teenagers can be very similar.

When you praise a three-year-old his face lights up and you can feel his pleasure. Praising a teenager doesn't always appear to have quite the same effect. You may be completely ignored, there may be a grunt, you might have it thrown back in your face or it might be accepted graciously. As a result, parents get out of the habit of praising older children. It may be that we think children don't need to be praised as they get older – certainly that seems to be the belief in school some schools. If you go into a nursery class, children will be praised constantly for any little achievement, but as children grow older there seems to be less and less praise around. In many lessons in secondary schools you will see and hear plenty of praise for good work, but virtually none for good behaviour and yet secondary school teachers cite bad behaviour as their number one cause of stress. Don't be fooled by their response – teenagers love being praised as much as the rest of us. Parents shouldn't stop praising just because teenagers don't seem to respond.

Once, when I was working as a behaviour consultant for a council in central London, I took a call from a senior education officer at the town hall, telling us we needed to drop everything and go to a secondary school which was in the middle of a crisis. When my colleague and I arrived no one was expecting us or had a clue as to what we were supposed to be doing. We tried to find the head, but he had disappeared. The school was a grim comprehensive with breeze-block, graffiti-covered corridors and teachers who looked wrung out. The behaviour was appalling, the children seemed to be pretty much in control of parts of the building and the atmosphere was bleak and depressing. We realised there were institutional problems that went way beyond our remit, but nevertheless we were obliged to spend three days there.

The relations between staff and pupils were pretty awful and they seemed to spend most of their time shouting at each other. Since no one had told us what to do, we decided to tour the building, smiling and saying *'Hello'* to the pupils and staff. So, for the rest of the first day we went round with fixed grins saying hello to everyone we met. I approached a group of scary-looking boys coming up a dark staircase, with the adrenalin pumping round my body.

'Hello,' I said.

One of them turned round menacingly. *'What did you say?'*

'I said hello.'

He looked at me suspiciously for a few seconds and then grunted, *'Hello.'*

I smiled at him, he smiled back at me and I walked off.

A few seconds later I heard another teacher come on to the scene.

'WHAT ARE YOU LOT DOING HERE? GET BACK TO YOUR CLASSES NOW!'

'But Sir, we were...' I heard my new friend splutter.

'ARE YOU ARGUING WITH ME? BACK TO CLASSES, NOW.'

Over the next three days we got to know a good proportion of the children and quite soon some of them started saying hello to us.

On our last day I was walking down the corridor with the head teacher, who we had finally managed to track down. He chivvied any children we came across. *'Come on, hurry up, you need to get to your next lesson.'* Or *'Hey you! Where's your tie?'*

We turned a corner and came across the group of boys I had met on my first day. Since our earlier encounter I had joined in with their basketball game at lunch time.

'Hello, Sir,' they said to me, smiling as they went past.

'How do you know that lot?' the head asked me suspiciously. *'They're a very nasty little bunch.'*

Teenagers want people to say nice things to them and to be praised when they get things right, despite the impression they can sometimes give.

How to Praise Teenagers

Praise is the most powerful tool parents have for improving their teenager's behaviour and raising their fragile self-esteem. It carries far more weight than a telling-off, shouting or imposing punishment. Parents don't always use praise effectively. Often parents tell their children that they are wonderful, amazing, incredible, fantastic... Hyperbole is at least positive and probably may help to lift morale (it's a lot better that being critical), however, as a currency this sort of praise soon gets devalued. Is a child really wonderful if she manages to finish her homework? Is it incredible to get out of bed in the morning? When a child receives this sort of praise he or she is left with a pleasant feeling that they have done something right, but they often don't know exactly what. This is especially confusing for teenagers who have been misbehaving, but just haven't been caught yet. *'Darling! You're wonderful!'* ends up being interpreted as *'Congratulations! You got away with it!'*

Teenagers are rightly cynical about this sort of praise and they will often ignore it.

Effective praise for teenagers is about letting them know what they have done right so they feel good about themselves and are more likely to repeat the behaviour. Praise works best when it is both specific and descriptive. The idea is that parents give a short description of what they are seeing and can then tag 'well done' on to the end.

'Well done for hanging your coat up.'

'You finished your homework, well done!'

Often, even 'well done' isn't necessary and sometimes the description is enough.

'You practised your trumpet hard tonight.'

'You left the bathroom clean.'

It is also useful to say *'thank you'* as a part of the praise.

'Thank you for coming back on time.'

'Thank you for asking so politely.'

'Thank you for being kind to your sister.'

Teenagers find this sort of praise much easier to accept than hyperbole, because it is honest and low-key.

Subjective praise is more loaded and it is not just teenagers who find it awkward. Give someone a subjective compliment about their new hair style, *'Your hair looks great'* and they often either discount it, *'Oh, I'm not really sure about it, I think it's a bit short'* or they refuse to accept it, *'I don't like it at all, I'm so disappointed.'*

When a friend or colleague gives you an opinion, you can decide whether you agree with it or not. When a parent merely describes the reality of what has just happened, it is impossible to deny. It is this sort of praise that will improve and consolidate teenagers' behaviour.

Praise the Effort

Telling children they are talented or good at something can often have the reverse effect. Labelling children, even in this positive way, actually reduces their confidence and their willingness to take risks. What is effective is when parents praise the effort their children have made. This encourages children to keep trying and to develop self-belief and reliance. So instead of saying, *'You are so talented at drawing, everything you do is brilliant'* say, *'Well done, you have worked really hard at drawing'* instead.

It is important not to sound sarcastic when giving praise. Teenagers often use sarcasm as part of their sense of humour and it is tempting to use it back to them, but praise must sound genuine. When parents praise they should not make reference to things that have gone wrong in the past and praise should never be qualified with a negative.

'Thanks for being polite today, unlike last week when you were a complete nightmare' is a really unhelpful way of praising. It's like a friend saying, *'That coat looks great, far better than that revolting one you usually wear.'*

If it is at all possible, parents should continue to offer hugs to their children as they become teenagers. Research suggests that parents who continue to cuddle, hug and kiss their teenagers will have fewer behaviour difficulties to contend with. Teenagers usually want that physical attention, but they are worried about seeming uncool and aren't very good at asking for it. They may find hugging embarrassing or uncomfortable or they may grow out of it, but parents can continue to make it available if their children need it.

Isn't it a Bit False?

Using the 6 to 1 ratio with children may sound contrived and even artificial at first. It is important that the praise is genuine, and there is no point in praising children for things they haven't done – you'll soon get rumbled. Descriptive praise is always genuine because it focuses on what the child has just done. It doesn't have to be something amazing or spectacular – the parent is simply noticing and commenting on something the child has done right, because she wants him to do it again.

Parents are often suspicious about giving out lots of praise. They think they will make their children spoilt and lacking in self-motivation. Praising is especially hard for parents who were themselves brought up in a low-praise environment, since we tend to base our parenting style on our own upbringing. This is particularly true for parents under stress – when challenged by their children's behaviour, they tend revert to using the same voice that their parents used with them.

Send Texts

One of the easiest and most effective ways of praising teenagers is by texting them. There is no embarrassing social interaction and it is hard to discount or reject the praise in a text message. Parents can send text messages when their child is away from the house and any tension that may be in the air. A quick *'Thank you'*, *'Well done'* or *'Congratulations'* will go down well and will give your child a little boost as he goes about his day. If he is the sort of child who finds praise particularly difficult to deal with, you can even text him when he is in his bedroom, and he'll be able to accept the praise without the cringe factor. He can respond if he wants to, but even if he doesn't you can be sure that the message is appreciated.

The Negative Cycle

Parents often get into a habit of constantly nagging their children. It's surprisingly easy to lose the habit of praising children when they behave well and to just focus on what is going wrong. When children do what they are supposed to, nothing gets said and the parents are just grateful that it's quiet for a minute. This means the currency of getting noticed by your parents becomes wholly negative. Children soon work out that if they want some attention then the best way of getting it is to misbehave. The child wants attention. She behaves well, no one notices. She behaves badly and everyone notices. It doesn't take long to learn the quickest route to get attention. It's depressing for parents who feel as if they spend their whole time nagging and it's depressing for the children, who get moaned at all the time.

Children can easily become stuck in the settled patterns of behaviour that have arisen between them and their parents. However unpleasant and damaging these patterns may be, the certainties of this action and reaction between parent and child may be more comfortable than fear of the unknown that comes with change. That is why parents and teenagers can so easily get locked into these damaging vicious cycles. It is as though the certainty of misery is better than the misery of uncertainty and both parties will often graduate back towards the status quo.

Let's look at how the 6 to 1 strategy helped Megan and Amy to get their relationship back on track.

Whatever, Mum!: A Case Study

Megan called me a couple of years ago about her daughter Amy, with whom she was having all kinds of difficulties. She talked about how unbelievably rude Amy was to her.

'She is almost incapable of being civil to me. When I ask her to do something she either ignores me or she makes such a fuss that it isn't worth the bother. She can barely make eye contact and she sighs constantly when I'm around. What is particularly annoying is that I hear her being sweet when she talks to her friends and the other day one of her friends' mother said how polite she was over at their house.'

It was obvious from talking to her that the two of them had got into a negative cycle. Whenever they had any contact, both of them were on their guard and ready for trouble. This state of mind is not conducive for a harmonious home. When people are in constant semi-reptile mode they find offence in the most innocuous conversation and misinterpret everything. Megan wanted to get her huge sense of frustration off her chest. She felt as if she did everything for her daughter and got nothing but rudeness in return. I have no doubt that Amy was probably feeling almost exactly the same way. Amy and her mother had forgotten what they liked about each other. This negative spiral is very common in the relationship between parent and teenager and if nothing is done, it can begin to have a serious effect on the atmosphere in the home. For things to change the impetus will have to come from the parent and this will often involve putting aside the intense annoyance she is feeling, taking a step back and planning to approach the problem from a new angle. Often the parent is feeling so cross and frustrated that this is the last thing she feels like doing and it will take a real effort of will.

Megan saw the logic of changing the way she reacted to Amy, but she was realistic about how difficult this was going to be. When I raised the issue of praise she said 'I do praise her all the time. I am constantly telling her how amazing she is and how much talent she has got and that if she doesn't use it, then it will all be wasted. All she does is swear at me.'

As this praise was random, unspecific and loaded with veiled criticism, it wasn't surprising that her daughter was unimpressed.

We wrote down a list of good things that Amy did. Megan was surprised by how long it was. It included:

- *Doing her own washing*
- *Keeping her room tidy*
- *Being nice to her little brother*
- *Usually coming back on time in the evenings*
- *Ringing to say if she is going to be late*
- *Being polite to her friends' parents (though Megan still found this hard to believe)*
- *Not smoking*
- *Being keen on environmental issues (but not able to turn any lights off)*
- *Doing her homework without being asked*
- *Getting good reports from school*
- *Getting up on school days with only a bit of fuss*

- *Eating properly*
- *Not being pregnant*

Once Megan got going she was able to come up with all kinds of things, especially when she thought of the things her friends were going through with their teenagers.

We then talked about how she could praise Amy for many of these qualities.

'What?' she said. 'You are seriously expecting me to turn round to my daughter and say "well done for not being pregnant"?'

I explained that she didn't have to praise every one of Amy's successes, but thinking about the things she is doing right, or not doing wrong, would put Megan into a more positive state of mind when it came to changing their behaviour. I asked her to practise giving praise in which she simply described what she saw.

I also talked about not relating the praise to any previous bad behaviour or there being any implied criticism, such as 'I wish you could always be as good as you are being today.'

I could feel there was still a lot of resistance. Megan was resentful of Amy and felt that the effort to praise more is very artificial. 'You are,' she said, 'expecting me to change the way I behave, when it's Amy who is being the pain and causing all the trouble.'

This feeling is common for the parents of many teenagers – criticising their children feels natural and genuine, but praising children seems false. It is, I explained, a question of mindset that very often comes from the parents' own upbringing and the way they were treated as children.

'You're certainly right about that. My mother criticised me constantly throughout my childhood.'

I persuaded her to at least try praising Amy more, and to concentrate on the way she spoke to Amy. Whenever Amy was polite, Megan was to comment on it in a low-key, positive way that couldn't be misinterpreted as being sarcastic or patronising. We practised a few expressions such as:

'Thank you for asking so nicely.'

'That smile really cheered me up.'

'Thank you for accepting me saying no, even though you really wanted to go out.'

'So polite!'

We also addressed the issue of Amy's rudeness. Megan agreed to try not to get hooked in by the way Amy spoke to her and to try and stay calm. When Amy was rude, Megan was either going to ignore her or calmly ask her to repeat whatever she had just said in an acceptable way. It was important that Megan was modelling the good manners she wanted to see from her daughter. We practised this a few times as I knew how easily Amy was able to get a reaction from her mother.

Finally I reminded Megan that she was going to have to be consistent with Amy and not give up.

Inevitably, Amy was going to be very suspicious about this change in attitude from her mother and was going to test out whether she was serious. I also said that at times Amy was going to get through Megan's defences and she was going to be able to provoke her. When this happened and Megan became angry, it was important that she wasn't too hard on herself or despaired and became tempted to give up.

Later that week I spoke to Megan. With Megan not getting hooked into arguments, the wind had been taken out of Amy's sails and she wasn't sure how to react. Her behaviour had been quite good, but Megan said the whole situation felt very artificial. It was, I explained, a sort of phoney war. Amy had noticed her mother being nicer and more appreciative towards her, but she wasn't convinced it was genuine and she hadn't yet decided how to react. I predicted that the next few days were going to be difficult as Amy was going to try and test her mother's commitment.

When we caught up later in the week, all hell had broken loose. Amy had thrown an almighty strop and called her mother every name under the sun. Somehow Megan had managed to stay calm, but she was seething with Amy and to some extent with me. I congratulated her for being strong and encouraged her to stick with it and keep going with the 6 to 1.

We spoke again three weeks later. I was worried that Megan wasn't going to be able to keep going and might have been tempted to give up and let things slip back into their previous, familiar pattern. My concern was unfounded. After a very difficult week, there had been a sea change in Amy's attitude and she was being far more polite. Megan was managing to keep up the level of praise and I was confident they would now be able to consolidate this new harmony. Having broken out of their previous cycle, things had now become easier. Megan was praising more, so Amy was feeling better. Because Amy was feeling better, her behaviour had improved. As a result of this improvement in behaviour Megan was feeling happier and was finding it easier to praise Amy. They were now caught in a virtuous circle that was going to become the new pattern for their relationship.

Like Megan, parents often find praising teenage children very difficult. The cocky, know-it-all attitude of many teenagers gives the impression that what they need is to be taken down a peg or two, rather than be praised. However, for much of the time, the last thing teenagers actually feel is cocky. This front is a defence that they put up to protect themselves from their lack of confidence. If parents think back to their own childhood they will recall that nagging sense of inadequacy that so often characterises the teenage years. Teenagers are expected to be grown up and show they can cope, so, on the surface they do so by striking this pose of arrogance and cool. Underneath it all, they are wracked by questions about who they are and where, if at all, they fit in. Parents have to see the child beyond the posturing and by praising they will help to build confidence, encourage better behaviour and attitude, and keep the relationship positive.

How to Use the 6 to 1 Strategy: A Summary

1. Using praise is the most effective way to improve and change behaviour.
2. To change behaviour parents should use the 6 to 1 praise-to criticism ratio.
3. Teenagers like being praised despite the impression they give. Don't stop praising just because they don't seem to like it.
4. Focus on the behaviour you want to see, not on what you don't want to see, and praise that behaviour whenever you notice it.
5. Avoid going over the top with praise – it's unnecessary and it doesn't feel genuine for teenagers. Keep it low key.
6. Praise that is subjective can be denied or thrown back, praise the effort not the outcome.
7. Praise is most effective when it is descriptive – simply praise what you see and say *'Thank you'*.

section three

tools for supporting better behaviour

6

rewarding your teenager

This chapter shows how the appropriate use of small rewards can help to improve teenagers' behaviour. It will help parents to avoid the pitfalls of over-rewarding, being inconsistent and ending up with children who become dependent on being rewarded. If used in conjunction with the 6 to 1 strategy, simple rewards will help to change the most difficult behaviours.

Why Should I Reward My Child For Doing What He Should Be Doing Anyway?

I am surprised by how many parents and teachers ask this question, getting hot under the collar at the idea of rewarding a child's good behaviour. The answer is because it works.

We are motivated by two types of reward. *Intrinsic*: the pride you feel when you achieve something such as learning to ride a bicycle, and *extrinsic*: a physical reward you get for doing something, such as being given a sweet by your mother when you learn to ride a bicycle. We bring children into a world in which extrinsic rewards for success are openly displayed, from Porsches to gold watches. We are all motivated by other people noticing our achievements and successes and children are no different.

How do you feel when nobody at work notices what a good job you are doing? If your boss puts a star-chart up in the boardroom and gave out certificates at the end of the week for the best employee, you would think it was infantile nonsense. However, despite yourself, you'd still get a little buzz when you got a star and you'd certainly notice who had won the certificate every week. We have an in-built need to be noticed and we like this need to be backed up by something tangible.

Imagine if your boss decided that, despite all the hard work you had put in over the year, there would be no Christmas bonus. After all, why do you need additional money for what you should be doing anyway? How would you feel if you didn't get a pay rise this year? If adults are motivated by such factors we can hardly be surprised that teenagers are as well, and as parents we can use this to our advantage.

We would love teenagers to need only intrinsic rewards, to do their homework on time purely for that sense of pride that comes with a job well done. The problem is that children do not have the foresight that adults have. Teenagers can't see that if they get out of bed on time, then they won't be late for school, they will be ready to learn, will pass their exams, will get into university, will get a good job, will be happy, successful and rich... Adults have this foresight and yet even we find it hard to always do what we ought to do. We all know that if we take more exercise and don't eat so much we will be healthier. Yet how many times did you go to the gym last month? Did you resist that chocolate biscuit? There is a constant tension within us between what we should do, what we want to do and what we can be bothered to do.

As we saw in the previous chapter, the good news is that the most effective reward of all for a teenager is free and easily to hand – praise. Simply noticing children doing the right thing will make them more likely to do it again. Sometimes, however, teenagers get into a pattern of behaviour that has become embedded and praise alone is not enough to do the job. The teenager may have begun to get some sort of pay-off for the behaviour, however negative it may seem, and it becomes necessary to use rewards to help to change things.

Rewarding teenagers is more complicated than it is with younger children. Even though they would almost certainly appreciate it, teenagers would be embarrassed to be given a sticker or a packet of sweets by their parents when they did something good. A well-thought out and consistent system of rewards, with lots of descriptive praise built in, will change the most ingrained, challenging pattern of behaviour. Rewards are a supremely useful tool in improving behaviour and they are a lot more fun to dish out than punishments.

What's the Difference Between a Reward and a Bribe?

Rewards are given by parents who are in control, to encourage the child to do the right thing. A reward is agreed in advance and given when the teenager does something positive. Bribes are given by parents who are not in control, to persuade the child to stop doing the wrong thing. The difference is subtle, but is of fundamental importance. Rewards encourage more good behaviour, bribes encourage more bad behaviour.

Making Rewards Work: The Five Golden Rules

1. *Use the reward to change one specific behaviour*
   When using rewards, focus on just one bit of behaviour you want to change. Don't be tempted to go for the most complicated or annoying, but choose something that would make everyone's life better if it changed. Tell the teenager specifically what you do want to see him doing, not what you don't want to see. Only give the reward for this behaviour, give it every time you see it and never give out the reward for anything else. If you start to give the reward for other 'good' things you will lose the focus and the system will founder.

2. *Keep the reward small*
   Parents often feel that they need to have a big, spectacular reward to motivate their teenager. This is not the case. What motivates the child is often not

the reward itself but the certainty that if he meets his target, he *will* get it.

Use little rewards to change little bits of behaviour. Remember, we want to change specific behaviour, we don't want perfect children.

3. *Make sure you deliver*

If your teenager has earned a reward, make sure he gets it. Parents seem to be hard-wired to notice their children when they are misbehaving, but when they are being good they can quickly fall off the radar. This means carefully planned reward systems can unravel because once the child has started to behave the rewards seem unnecessary to the parent and they dry up. The message to the teenager is therefore *this isn't really that important.* If this happens before the good behaviour has become ingrained, then it is likely the teenager will slip back to his old ways.

4. *Make it time-limited*

If you focus on changing one particular piece of behaviour, it shouldn't take more than a month at most. If you haven't seen a substantial change in that time, your target is almost certainly too difficult for the child and you will need to think again.

The first week should see the teenager enthusiastic about winning the reward and it will often go very well. During the second week, the teenager will often try out the old behaviour to see how serious you are about change. The third week, things will start to really change and the fourth week gives a chance for the new behaviour to become embedded. Once this has happened, you can both formally end the reward and target. Parents often keep the reward system going for ages because they think stopping may cause the child to go back to the old behaviour. This is rarely the case. Once the pattern has been broken, it doesn't usually restart, and in any case, children usually appreciate the new positive outcome and are ready to move on. Bear in mind that, despite appearances to the contrary, teenagers don't want to be in trouble all the time, they just get stuck, along with their parents, in a negative pattern. If you let a reward system go on too long it loses its impact, the parent gets bored and the child loses interest in the reward.

5. *Don't mess with rewards*

Never take away rewards from teenagers as a punishment. Rewards are earned and once earned need to be delivered. This is why they work best when they are focused on specific behaviour – when you see that behaviour, they get the reward. This can be galling when your teenager is earning his reward, but being obnoxious in all sorts of other ways. Remember you are not trying to change everything at once and if he is succeeding with his target behaviour then you are making progress.

Don't have one of those *Right!* moments when you tell your teenager you are cancelling the reward because he is being such a pain, however exasperated you are. If you do, all the hard work that you and your child have put in will be lost.

Choosing a Reward

Choosing a reward that will be acceptable and keep your child motivated is a challenge. Often the best thing to do is to ask your teenager what he would like. Usually, to parents' surprise, they come up with something modest and reasonable. Children will be far more motivated to work towards something they have chosen rather than a reward that has been imposed on them.

Here are some rewards that I have found effective with teenagers.

Money

Money is the most effective reward for teenagers. They are usually broke and there is always something they want to buy. Parents need to work out what is a reasonable amount of money to offer as a reward, taking into account the amount of pocket money their teenager usually receives, as well as their age. Don't be tempted to offer large amounts of money as a reward. It isn't necessary. The reward simply needs to be a large enough proportion of the teenager's pocket money to motivate him. Try to keep the reward as small as possible – you don't want to bankrupt yourself in order to persuade your teenager to finish his homework without moaning. Remember, even though your teenager won't admit it, the recognition and praise from you will be as motivating as the cash.

Time

Teenagers are always trying to negotiate over time. They want to stay out later, spend the night at a friend's house, put off doing their homework and delay writing a thank-you letter to their grandmother. Parents can take advantage of this by rewarding good behaviour with the offer of more time. If a teenager reaches his behaviour target he can earn the right to come home half an hour later or go out with his friends for a day. It is worth noting that time will only work as a reward if there is a fairly tight curfew already in place. If the return time is up for negotiation every night then the reward will be meaningless. In addition, parents can offer their own time as a reward. Many teenagers seem hell-bent on trying to get away from their parents, but they may actually like spending time with them if they can agree on something they all like doing. The possibility of being taken on a shopping trip can be a big motivator for a teenager, but the parent has to be prepared not to take their child if they don't make the target.

Things

As an alternative to money, parents can offer tangible rewards. These can include vouchers, DVDs, CDs, books and clothes. Again, keep the reward relatively small. If it costs too much then you may not be quite as keen for your child to earn it.

Big Stuff

Parents often offer large rewards that are earned for good behaviour over a long period of time, such as a new iPod or a holiday. In general, I am not keen on this system because it seems to be more about paying the child to be good, rather than about changing or improving behaviour. Rewards that offer a fantastic prize in the distant future seem alluring, but they are too remote to affect the day-to-day behaviour of children. I don't think parents should use rewards simply to keep their child on the straight and narrow. This leads to children becoming motivated only by the material reward and failing to develop an intrinsic sense of achievement.

I believe rewards are for changing behaviour and once the behaviour has changed then the reward is no longer necessary.

Potential Pitfalls

Over-rewarding

Don't fall into the pitfall of over-rewarding. If your child is expecting to get 50 pence when he completes his homework then it must be no more than 50 pence. If you hand out two pounds because you are in a good mood and your teenager is being less annoying than usual, then you devalue the process.

Siblings

When you are trying to change the behaviour of one of your children, it can often cause jealousy and resentment among their siblings, particularly if the children are close in age. Often simply explaining that you are using the rewards to help change the sibling's behaviour is enough.

The alternative is to set a target for the sibling to work on as well. It may be that there isn't something obvious, but if you ask the child he will usually think of something he would like to improve. They can earn their own rewards separately from each other without needing to be jealous. It is important to avoid negative comparisons, such as *'Well, your brother earned 50 pence today, but you aren't going to.'*

Unachievable Rewards

I recently came across a father who had told his son that if he could be polite for a whole week he would take him to a football match. The reward had been on offer for the whole season, but his son had never achieved it. This father had missed the point of rewarding behaviour completely. It is *essential* that the reward is attainable and the teenager gets it regularly. An unachievable reward has no motivational power and does nothing for your child's self-esteem. The reward is dangled over him as a constant reminder of his failure.

Unreasonable Expectations

Take into account the age and maturity of your teenager when you set a reward target. Just because an older sibling could meet the target when he was a similar age, does not mean all your children can. If you set a reward system up and the teenager is not earning rewards, then you have set the bar too high and you are expecting too much. Just because they *should* be able to make the target at their age, it does not mean they *can*. Choose something they definitely can achieve if they make an effort.

Think of a comparison with reading. We wouldn't expect a child who has just learnt the alphabet to tackle *War and Peace*, and we shouldn't have unreasonable expectations of their behaviour either.

After one successful campaign against a particular bit of bad behaviour, it is tempting to go straight into another against another problem: resist. Take a good few weeks out before you decide to have a go with another bit of behaviour. If the reward doesn't feel fresh and exciting then it won't work nearly as well.

Successful reward systems also have a positive effect on parents. They help parents to focus on what is going well, rather than on what is going badly, and quite naturally increase the praise-to-criticism ratio to nearer 6 to 1.

The following case study shows the importance of rewards and how they can give an extra push to change a situation that has become horribly stuck.

Laura and Alice: A Case Study

Laura, the mother of 14-year-old Alice, contacted me about her daughter's rudeness. Whenever she was asked to do anything Alice had got in the habit of answering back and arguing. This sent Laura into full reptile mode and they ended up having a blazing row. Alice had remarkable staying power and at the end of these exchanges she still wanted to have the last word, either a semi-audible insult muttered under her breath or a five-star teenage tantrum. Their relationship had become very strained and there was a palpable tension in the house whenever Alice was around.

When I visited the home I witnessed the conflict first hand. Alice had decided that she needed to go shopping that afternoon because she had planned to go to the cinema with her friends and she had nothing to wear. Her mother tactfully tried to point out that she had so many clothes that it had become impossible to shut her wardrobe. This did not go down well. Alice did a few textbook teenage huffs and puffs and then swept out of the room. Three minutes later she was back.

'If,' she wailed, the tears welling up in her eyes, 'if you could just stop putting yourself first for once in your life, you could see that I don't have any of the things my friends have. You haven't seen the looks they give me when I turn up in the same clothes day after day. But you don't care because you're too busy thinking about yourself.' Her rant was beginning to warm up. 'You never give me any support, you never say anything nice to me. The others get all your time and attention, but you never give me anything.'

She was beginning to press Laura's buttons now and Laura began to react.

'Excuse me? I never give you any support? What about ferrying you around four nights a week so you can keep up with your busy social life? Who rang up your school the other day and made up some story to get you off the hook because you couldn't be bothered to do your homework? Who cooks and cleans for you like a slave because you are supposedly working so hard, even though I know you spend most of your time on Facebook?'

They were in free-flowing reptile mode and both seemed to have forgotten that I was in the room. The tunnel vision that came from their flight-or-fight reaction meant they were locked into the conflict to the exclusion of the outside world.

'I hate you, I hate you,' screamed Alice through her tears, and for the second time she made a theatrical exit. He mother slumped into a chair and wept silently for a few minutes until she remembered I was there and started trying to apologise.

'I'm so sorry, she gets to me every time. I always say I won't let it happen, but she has a way of getting right under my skin that means I react every time.'

The two of them had got into a pattern that was going to be difficult to unravel. Alice was getting some sort of psychological pay off by picking fights with her mother. I felt she was probably suffering from the sort of low self-esteem that affects so many teenagers (the line about the looks she was getting from her friends was a bit of a giveaway). Rowing with her mother was a way of confirming her feelings of worthlessness. 'Even my mother doesn't like me' is a highly destructive way of behaving, but it is curiously hard to escape. This pattern is common in many teenagers who become trapped in a vicious cycle of behaviour that affirms their negative view of the world and their place in it.

What Alice needed was affirmation and support to help her feel better about herself, but the behaviour pattern she was locked into made it increasingly difficult for her mother to get through to her. Laura had been on the end of some undermining abuse that had left her understandably resentful. Laura knew that she would have to find a way of not getting pulled into arguments with her daughter, at the same time as helping her to change her self-image.

I got Laura to work out some scripts to use when she could feel Alice was picking a fight or being unreasonable. She chose to say 'I'm sorry that you don't like my decision, but I'm sticking to it' and 'I know it's really annoying for you, but I have decided this is how we are going to do it.' Laura said it felt very artificial for her to be rehearsing lines that she was going to use in a future argument, but I explained that the reptile brain stops any rational thought and the best way of dealing with an emotional threat is to have a plan in place that can be drawn on without needing to think about it. I then got her to imagine putting on a defensive cloak that would protect her from the insults that Alice would use to try and get her to change her mind and come away from this new, calm position Laura was taking up. The idea seemed ludicrous to her, but I explained that imagining a physical barrier to words can be a real help in deflecting words that are designed to hook us in.

Once we had worked out Laura's new, more resilient responses to Alice, then we looked at changing Alice's behaviour. I asked Laura what she wanted to change most about Alice and what she wanted to see instead. Without hesitation, she said her habit of answering back and arguing. Laura wanted Alice to be able to accept 'no' without starting a battle and to express her feelings of disappointment without being rude.

The behaviour was so stuck in its pattern that I thought it would need the extra push of a reward to kick-start the change. Laura would offer to take Alice shopping the next weekend and during the trip she would find an opportunity to talk about Alice's behaviour and how she wanted things to be different.

'I don't think I can do that,' said Laura, 'I am just too cross with her to be able to do it.'

I understood where she was coming from but I said Laura was going to have to make the first move. If she was hoping Alice was going to get out the peace pipe, then she was going to be in for a long wait. An unearned gesture of kindness was going to be the first step on the road to harmony. Next we discussed how we could reward Alice when she was polite and accepted the word 'no'.

'I can't give her something every time she is polite,' Laura said.

I asked why not and Laura replied that felt this was going over the top. I explained that the reward didn't have to be big. If they were going to escape this cycle, they were going to have to punctuate every success with something nice. I didn't want to use money because I felt we could get into a situation in which Alice's manners were only dependent on cash.

I suggested using shopping tokens, a reward I had used with a young teen in the past. Whenever Alice was able to accept 'no' or was polite, she would be given a shopping token. Each token had a different value written on the back and Alice had no way of knowing which was which. Most were worth 20 pence but there were a few more valuable ones, up to the value of five pounds. At the weekend Alice could choose to go shopping or bank the money and go at a later date. The randomness of the tokens was designed to keep Alice's interest and enthusiasm up, without costing her mother too much. The only rule was that Alice would have to go on these shopping trips with her mother – part of the plan was that they spent some quality time together. Laura designed some tokens on the computer and printed them off. She took 20 pounds' worth with her on her goodwill shopping trip the first weekend to supplement Alice's meagre savings. She would present them to Alice at the same time as she introduced the new rules and reward system. Before I left I reminded Laura not to supplement the tokens with extra handouts if Alice found something she couldn't quite afford, as this would undermine the value of the rewards. I also explained that when Alice did decide to go shopping, Laura should find the time as soon as possible. The longer the delay, the less Alice would associate the reward with her good behaviour.

Finally, I prepared Laura for some resistance from Alice. Asking Alice to change her behaviour was going to take her out of her comfort zone and she was going to test Laura to see if she was really serious.

I spoke to Laura a week later and she was on a real high. The shopping trip had been a great success. Laura and Alice had lunch together and Laura handed over the tokens and explained what they were for. They then spent the afternoon trying on clothes and spending the money.

'We were actually laughing together, we haven't done that for two years,' Laura told me. Over the course of the day she had given out more tokens when Alice did what she was asked. Since then things had gone pretty well. Alice had one big blip when Laura wouldn't let her go out because her homework wasn't finished, but she put on the defensive cloak and managed to stick to her guns without biting back.

I saw Laura one more time about a month later. Things were by no means perfect and Alice could still be very difficult at times, but they were getting on so much better. Laura felt that whatever happened from now she would be able to deal with it and stay in control. I suggested that they give the tokens a couple more weeks and then stop them altogether. Laura was reluctant to do this, as the tokens had been the salvation of her relationship with her daughter. I felt that the behaviour had changed and Alice didn't need to be kept on such a tight rein. Also, there was a danger that the token idea may start to become a bit stale. Instead, I advised her to congratulate Alice on doing so well and increase her pocket money to make up for the ending of the tokens. The message this sent was, 'Well done for changing your behaviour. Now you can decide how you spend your money.' When I talked to Laura again she said Alice was continuing to do well and she was insisting that the two of them continued to go shopping together.

Rewarding Your Teenager: A Summary

1 Teenagers can't see the long-term effects of behaving well. Rewards help them to get back on track in the short term. Change won't always be instant and parents will need to keep going, even when they don't seem to be getting anywhere.

2 Rewards should be used to change one specific piece of behaviour at a time. Only reward that behaviour. Don't give out rewards for other things, however good the child is being, as you will water down the impact of the reward.

3 Rewards should be small, cheap and easy to administer. Don't be afraid to give out lots at first. Your teenager has to see quickly what is in it for him.

4 It is not the size of the reward but the certainty of receiving it that will change behaviour.

5 Children should receive rewards as soon as possible after the good behaviour, otherwise the impact is lost.

6 *Never, ever, ever, take rewards away.* If the child has earned the reward by achieving the target you agreed, he must get it. You can delay the delivery if he is being a real pain, but he really should get it sooner rather than later.

7

punishments and consequences

When I worked in a comprehensive school in London, there seemed to be two ways of disciplining the children. The first was for a teacher to stick his face about one inch away from a child's and shout at the top of his voice like an American marine sergeant. The second was to hand out a detention. A fair proportion of pupils seemed to get bawled at every day and then have to spend an hour after school sitting in detention.

There is a depressing slide towards ever more punitive behaviour management as children move up the education system. In nurseries there are high levels of praise and positive reinforcement, but by the time children get to secondary school, all too often the only praise they ever get is for their work. There is an expectation that they will behave well and when they don't they just get punished. Persistently punishing children does little to change their behaviour – look at the pupils at that comprehensive school who were in detention every night.

Parents can also get stuck in this mindset. When their child was a toddler being potty trained, we would have heard constant praise for every effort the child made, backed up with stickers and rewards. By the time that child is a gangly teenager, all that praise can dry up. Many parents get into the same cycle as the teachers at my old school. Punishment is layered upon punishment and the teenager has nothing left to motivate him. If you are grounded for two months, effectively your life has been taken away from you and there is little incentive to behave.

That is not to say I am against teenagers facing consequences for their behaviour. They need to know what the rules are and to understand that if they go too far, or their behaviour becomes unacceptable, then there will be repercussions. However, punishments are only really effective in a system that shows teenagers how they are supposed to behave (rather than how not to behave) and praises and rewards them when they manage it.

The difficulty for parents is that when their child misbehaves they can easily slip into reptile mode and start handing out draconian punishments because they are angry. When teenagers are misbehaving, punishing them can make parents feel strong and powerful, but the short-term control they gain at these moments can end up feeding into the pattern that makes their child misbehave.

The Punishment Cycle: A Case Study

Geoff had got himself stuck in a complete rut with his 15-year-old son Jason.

'He seems to be on a mission to wind me up. He ignores virtually anything I ask him to do, unless I really yell at him. He comes and goes as he pleases and I have the school ringing up most afternoons telling me about his latest scrape. Last week it was his course work that hadn't appeared on time; the week before, he had been smoking and next week, who knows what? We have now reached the stage where I have run out of things to take away from him, but he is still doing exactly what he wants. He has no pocket money till the end of the month for the smoking, he is grounded for the next three weeks because he kept missing his curfew times, I have taken the TV out of his room because he wasn't going to bed on time and I have confiscated his laptop because he plays video games and watches porn when he should be working. Short of emptying his wardrobe or taking the sheets off his bed, there is nothing else I can do.'

Geoff had got himself into a difficult position. He had given out some severe consequences while in reptile mode and did not want to appear weak by backing down.

'Part of me would like to let him off some of this, but I think that will just make him push it even more. Give him an inch and he will take a mile.'

I sympathised with the difficult position that Geoff found himself in. Jason had nothing left to lose and if Geoff's authority was based on his ablilty to find punishments to keep his son in control, then he was quickly reaching the end of the runway. He was beginning to accept that what he was doing wasn't working. I managed to convince him that he would have to find a way of reducing some of the punishments without losing too much face. Geoff and I went to his local pub where we wouldn't be able to hear Jason's music and made a plan over a couple of pints.

We decided to wipe the slate clean for Jason and give him a fresh start.

Geoff would sit down and talk to him calmly and explain that he felt they had both dug themselves into a hole and that because things had got so tricky they were going to start again from scratch. I tried to persuade Geoff that this was a strong thing to do because he was showing his son that he could acknowledge that things weren't working. He wasn't entirely convinced, but he was prepared to swallow his pride and take the risk.

'It couldn't get any bloody worse!' he conceded.

We then worked out what behaviour Geoff wanted to see from Jason. This took some time because he was so stuck in a negative spiral he couldn't imagine Jason being good. In the end we decided to focus on getting his homework done and meeting curfews. We made half of Jason's pocket money dependent on finishing his homework and getting back on time in the evening. I didn't want to link all the pocket money to his behaviour because I wanted him to have something left even if he messed up completely. We then worked out a list of suitable consequences that were as much as possible linked to the crime:

- *Jason was not allowed to play on his computer or watch television until all his homework was completed for the night and checked by his father.*

- *For every five minutes Jason was late for his curfew, he would have to be back half an hour earlier the next time.*

This second consequence had to be quite harsh in order to be enough to convince Jason to turn away from his friends and get home on time, despite the powerful pull of FOMO. Geoff was keen to create a list of punishments for every conceivable misdemeanour, but I reminded him we were just going to focus on these two problem areas first. I also talked about the importance of praising Jason, even if he didn't appear to take any notice.

The next stage was for Geoff to sit down with his son and talk through the plan. I was hoping that Jason would accept the clean slate as a peace offering and be prepared to give the new system a go.

When I met Geoff for a pint a couple of weeks later he couldn't wait to tell me how well things were going. To his amazement, Jason had been back on time every night, and Geoff was letting him stay out an extra half an hour in the evenings. The negative cycle had been broken and the relationship was back on course. There had been some hiccups with the homework, especially when Geoff had work commitments and wasn't there to supervise. However, most of the homework was being done most of the time, which was a big improvement on what was going on before.

'It's all so much better,' said Geoff, draining his glass, 'but now he wants to stay in the house on his own when we go away next weekend. I don't know if I can trust him ...'

Geoff and I had been able to stop the punishment cycle and introduce some logical consequences for Jason that, along with rewards and praise, lead to a breaking down of the pattern that had built up between them. By focusing on just two areas of behaviour, Geoff was able to concentrate his energies on making sure Jason got those right, rather than having to firefight every piece of bad behaviour that came along. Jason was not going to be perfect, but the two of them had affected enough change to keep their relationship on an even keel.

5 Golden Rules for Punishments and Consequences

1. *Plan them in advance*
Work out suitable consequences in advance, so that when you are in reptile mode you don't come out with something absurdly unfair and draconian.

2. *Keep them small*
Bigger, more dramatic punishments won't change behaviour. They will cause resentment from your

child. Teenagers who have lost all their privileges have nothing left to lose and parents run out of leverage. More important than the size of the consequence is the certainty that you will follow through. If your teenager does something wrong and you have threatened a consequence, then it must happen. If you are haphazard or erratic, then the message is that the bad behaviour matters more on some days than on others, such as when you are in a bad mood or when you have the energy to make a fuss.

3. *Use sparingly*

If you need to punish your child the whole time then something is not right. How much praise and positive attention are you giving out? Have you considered using rewards? Do you need to spend some time teaching your teenager how you want her to behave? Are your expectations too high?

4. *Make the punishment fit the crime*

Try to link the consequence to the bad behaviour. If your child has come in too late in the evening, then make him come back earlier next time. If he leaves the kitchen in a state, get him to clean it up.

5. *Delay before you punish*

When teenagers have just done something particularly annoying, try to avoid giving out a punishment on the spot. In reptile mode you are likely to come out with an over-the-top sanction that you will regret. Say something like, 'We'll discuss this later,' and give yourself a bit of time to think things through. Often parents may find the real source of their irritation at that moment was nothing to do with their child. Getting cross about teenage behaviour can be an outlet for adults' anger or frustration about other issues.

Effective Consequences

Grounding

This punishment is commonly used by parents as a way of keeping control over their teenagers. Parents often ground their children for weeks at a time, meaning the child has nothing to look forward to and little motivation to behave. This can lead to a cycle of misbehaviour and grounding that means the teenager doesn't get to go out for months, with neither parent nor child being able to remember the original reason. Grounding is more effective when it is used sparingly. Preventing your child from going out for one evening is enough to show your disapproval and your refusal to accept his poor behaviour.

Try to use grounding when it is a logical consequence to the original bad behaviour. For example, *'You went round to your friend's house after school without checking with me. I need to be able to trust you, if you do it again then you won't be able to go out on Saturday night'* or '*If you are rude to me, then I won't feel like giving you a lift to the party this weekend, which will mean you can't go.'*

Try to avoid a *'RIGHT'* moment halfway through October. *'Right, that's it, you're grounded till Christmas!'*

Docking Pocket Money

Most teenagers are broke, so threatening to dock some of their pocket money is a good way of keeping them on the straight and narrow. Don't be tempted to take away the lot, a few pence or a couple of pounds is enough. If you take too much away, your teenager is likely to feel so resentful that he won't learn from the experience. Remember, the point of a punishment is to get him to think before he mucks up again, not to get even with him.

Removing Electrical Stuff

If your teenager is consistently playing his music too loudly and does not respond to a warning, then it makes sense to remove his hi-fi for a couple of days. Children who are spending their time on social networking sites or gawping at YouTube when they should be working, could have their computer removed for a short period of time. The same could go for television, if they have one.

Punishments and Consequences: A Summary

1. Punishing teenagers can make parents feel strong and in control, though in reality it can often make things worse and sour the relationship between parent and child.
2. Punishments alone won't change bad behaviour. Make it clear to your child what you want him to do, then praise and, if necessary, reward him.
3. Keep punishments as small as possible. What changes behaviour is the certainty, after the threat, of getting the consequence, not the size of the punishment.
4. Whenever possible give children a warning before you hand out a consequence.
5. The objective of a consequence is to show your child that the bad behaviour is unacceptable and to encourage him not to do it next time. It is not a means for you to get even.

8

hard cases

This chapter is like one of those alarms that say *In case of fire break glass.* If you do decide to use the techniques here, there will be a lot of noise and potentially some broken glass to clear up. The advice in this chapter is to be used when parents feel they have lost all authority over their teenager and things are getting desperate. It follows a tight programme that will help the parent to re-establish control. For the process to be successful parents will need to be determined and committed. The reality is that it is difficult to turn around the behaviour of a teenager who has gone off the rails. There is a temptation to give up when things don't initially work out. It is essential that parents back each other up and commit together to bring about change.

What is a Hard Case?

A hard case will mean different things to different people. Individual parents will know if they have a hard case on their hands. Periods of conflict are an inevitable part of parenting teenagers. At some stage, most children will try and push the boundaries. Hard cases are teenagers who don't seem to stop pushing and where every interaction between parent and child involves conflict. They are children who fail to submit to the most basic rules of the home and live a parallel existence to the rest of the family. One parent described it as *'like having a delinquent ghost in the house who appeared in the night, raided the fridge and my purse and then floated off leaving a faint smell of socks and marijuana in his wake.'* I think it is the combination of the frequency and the intensity of the bad behaviour that turns a normal teenager into a hard case.

Many teenagers are abusive to their parents, but few are abusive all the time. Parents of hard cases will feel overwhelmed by what they are having to deal with and there is often a real temptation to simply give up and let the child do what he or she wants. Other factors that define a hard case are drugs, alcohol, stealing, smoking and sex. Most children will try most of these at some stage, but the hard cases start early and rather than just dipping their toe in the water, they plunge in head first at every opportunity.

Can Life Improve?

The answer is yes, but it is going to be hard work. Part of the process will be to unravel some complex behaviour patterns that have grown up in both the parent and the child. For some parents it is hard, or even impossible, to accept the idea that you will have to change in order to help your child to change. Put simply, if you do what you have always done, then you will get what you have always got. It is not helpful for parents to spend hours pondering how they have got into this situation, nor do I want to make them feel any guiltier than they almost certainly are feeling already. However, parents must be prepared to recognise that they played their part in the process of the deterioration of their child's behaviour and that they need to play a major part in the resolution. If there is a real commitment to make things better, then hard cases can soften.

Parents must be mindful of their emotions and the way they can feed the behaviour patterns. In order to regain authority, parents must avoid being drawn in by their child's behaviour. Many parents in this situation will be feeling so cross with their child that, though they love him, they are finding it very hard to like him. One father told me about a time he was looking at photos on the computer. *'A picture of my 14-year-old son came up on the screen and I immediately got butterflies in my stomach.'* The conflict with his son was so bad that a photograph was enough to send him into reptile mode.

The Reward and the Sanction

Money is going to be both the reward and the sanction in changing behaviour in hard cases.

Remember, we are trying to undo some ingrained and difficult patterns here, so parents will have to put aside some of their reservations about whether it is appropriate to use money in this context. The answer to any doubts is that it works.

The first thing is to audit what money you give your child. This needs to take into account everything he gets. Some children will receive pocket money; others will have an allowance that goes towards paying for clothes, mobile phones and so on. It doesn't matter which system you are using but there must be absolute consistency. Do not give out cash on a whim. This strategy will not succeed if there is any fluctuation in how much you give your child. You cannot have a set amount of pocket money and then give him a handout for a new CD because he is being particularly sweet and has asked so nicely. Your partner must also commit to this programme. There is no point in you sticking tightly to the plan if your husband or wife (or grandparent) is bunging your child a tenner whenever they see him. If your child is getting money or lots of presents from elsewhere then you will have to cut off the supply. He won't be motivated by earning his pocket money if there are lots of other streams of revenue. To change your child's behaviour you will need to set a weekly rate and stick to it.

Decide What You Want to Change

When you have a child who has become a hard case it will feel as though he never does anything right. Parents can feel overwhelmed by the conflict when the problem seems too big to change. The secret is to choose one thing about your child that you would like to change and make this your focus. It doesn't necessarily have to be the worst thing. What parents will find is that if they can change one thing, then they will have the confidence and authority to work on other problems. In my experience, parents often choose manners or communication, but coming home on time is also a common issue. Once you have decided on your issue, think about what you would like to see instead. For parents who feel stuck in a negative spiral this can be a difficult exercise. Sometimes things have got so bad that they can't imagine an alternative. If you are in this state, try to envisage how things would be if they were perfect, what you would do, what your child would be doing. In this fantasy situation what would a camera filming in the house record? I once worked with a mother who was in such a state about her daughter that the most positive outcome she could imagine was for her to be '*not quite so rude*'. When I suggested '*How about her being polite?*', she said, '*Oh no, I'm never going to make her polite.*'

She was wrong. Six weeks later her daughter was a changed girl – polite, friendly and even charming at times.

Parents need to have a clear idea of the positive behaviour that they want to see, so they are ready to give out praise for it. This is the basis for the programme of changing specific negative behaviour for hard cases.

Turning Money into Behaviour Units

The next thing is to divide your child's weekly pocket money into behaviour tokens. In order to take back control you are going to need to use all the leverage you can, and money is one of the most powerful. Divide his weekly rate by seven to get a daily rate and then divide this by twenty to give you the value of his behaviour tokens. Here is an example to make things clear.

Tom, aged 15, gets 14 pounds a week in pocket money that means he gets a daily rate of two pounds. This is then divided by 20, meaning the value of a behaviour token for Tom is 10 pence. It is not helpful to be dealing in individual pennies so round the pocket money up or down to the nearest 10 pence. Then you need to go to the bank and get lots of change. If the behaviour token is ten pence then you need to get a large stash of 10 pence coins. The programme will stand or fall on you being prepared.

How the Tokens Work

You have chosen one part of your child's behaviour that you are committed to changing. This is the only behaviour you are going to focus on for the first few weeks.

Your child has a maximum of 20 tokens he can forfeit during the course of the day. Every time he misbehaves in the specific area you are focusing on, you tell him he has lost a token. At the end of the day, or first thing the next morning, you give him all the tokens/money that are left. If he has misbehaved 12 times then, then in our example above, he will have earned 80 pence.

The Conversation

This is when you are going to explain the new regime to your child. You need to find a moment when you are both relatively calm. It can be useful to make some kind of peace offering to get him on your side, such as making his favourite tea. It is also useful to practise the conversation in advance. You want to be outlining in a dispassionate way what the problem is, what you want to see instead and how you are going to use the behaviour tokens to make progress. Having a script will help you to stick to the point and stay calm, whatever his reaction. Here is an example.

> *'Hi Tom, I want to have a quick chat about how things are at the moment. This isn't going to be a telling off, I just want to make a plan so we can make things better. The issue I have is the way you are speaking to me at the moment. It feels like every conversation we have turns into a row and I find some of the things you say very rude.* [Using 'I' here works well. You are saying what you feel and he can't argue with how his behaviour makes you feel.] *For example, the other day when I asked you to tidy your room, you shouted back, "Fuck off and tidy it yourself".* [The memory of such events may start to send you into reptile mode. The rehearsal will stop this from happening.] *Rather than shouting all the time I want you to answer me politely when I ask you something. When you want something from me, you need to ask in the right way. I know at times I have been shouty with you and I am going to try to stop doing that as well.'* [Some acknowledgement of your own failings is useful as it pre-empts him having a go at you and shows you are in reconciliatory mode.]

Give your teenager the opportunity to have his say. It is useful for both of you to clear the air at the beginning of the process. He may have suggestions of his own. If these are reasonable, then it will be helpful to incorporate them into the plan. The more the teenager feels part of the process, the more likely it is to succeed.

Then explain the new token system to him.

> *'I have divided your daily pocket money up into 10 pence pieces. Every time you are rude to me you will lose 10 pence. Every morning I will give you the pocket money you have earned the previous day. If you go over your daily rate then you will lose money off the next day's quota. You will probably think I am being over the top and horrible, but things need to change.* [Acknowledgement of his feelings.] *I know this is a big change. Is there anything you would like to ask?'*

How this conversation goes will depend on both your moods and the current state of the relationship, but it is important to get your message across clearly and not to be sidetracked. You have made the decision to go down this road and the most likely cause of failure is if you don't stick to it.

How the Tokens Work

The tokens work because they help to take the emotional component out of dealing with bad behaviour. Usually when a parent has a problem with a teenager they deal with it by telling the child off. This can take the form of snapping, shouting, arguing, trying to make the child feel guilty or attempting to have a conversation about why the behaviour is unacceptable. There is almost inevitably an emotional component to telling a child off. The parent is often annoyed, disappointed or angry and the child reacts to these feelings and often returns them with interest. For many children, being told off gives them the attention that they crave. The parent and child have got stuck in such a negative cycle that being told off is the predominant, and sometimes the only, way the child can get attention. By using tokens the parent is able to notice and deal with the behaviour without emotion. Each time the parent sees the specific behaviour they calmly say what has happened and they let the child know he has lost a token. *'Tom, because you have answered back rudely, you have lost a token.'*

If he continues to be rude then he will lose another one. Most children will attempt to argue and parents can easily get sidetracked.

> *'Mum, I didn't answer back rudely, I was being polite.'*
>
> *'Excuse me! I think muttering under your breath is very rude.'*
>
> *'It wasn't, I didn't hear you properly. You are being so unfair.'*
>
> *'I am not being unfair. You were rude so you have lost a token.'*

This could easily turn into a full-blown argument and the original problem will have been completely forgotten. By arguing, the child has deflected the parent and the conversation has become emotional, which is exactly what we want to avoid. Rather than argue, simply say, *'It's my decision'* and leave it at that. Part of this process is developing the parent's authority without being macho or aggressive.

The tokens also help to promote consistency in the parent. One of the reasons for so much conflict can be the different responses parents give to similar behaviour. On one day the parents will tell the child off calmly; on another day they may shout; on other occasions parents can be so worn out that they let the behaviour go without comment. The child receives mixed messages about the behaviour. Is it serious? Does it matter? Consequently there is little change. By using the tokens, the parents are being clear about giving the same consequence for the same behaviour each time it happens.

It is absolutely essential that the child receives the full daily value of his remaining tokens either before bed or first thing the next morning. This means parents must have the coins ready to make the payment. As soon as the parents start writing IOUs or paying up only at the end of the week, they are sending a message that they are not serious about the process. The child will pick up on this and the motivation for change will disappear. If the deal is that the child will get his money first thing in the morning then he must receive it, otherwise the link between the behaviour and the reward and sanction has gone. Think of the cash the child receives as money earned, not as money that hasn't been lost. As his behaviour improves, the child will earn more, he will feel rewarded and motivated by both the money and the sense of achievement.

Praise the Achievements

Part of the success of the tokens relies on rebooting the relationship between the parents and the child and healing much of the pain and anguish that has been caused by the teenager getting out of control. The most effective way of promoting this is for the parents to use a very high level of praise. In Chapter 5, I focused on how to praise teenagers effectively using the 6 to 1 strategy. By noticing what your child is doing well you are encouraging more of the behaviour you want to see. If we are taking tokens away when they are doing the wrong thing, then we must balance this by commenting when they are doing things right. Achieving a 6 to 1 praise-to-criticism ratio is extremely difficult when you have a teenager who has become a hard case, but this difficulty is precisely the reason why parents need to persevere and stay positive. The relationship has become so strained that it has become hard to use praise, the most effective tool in helping children to behave. However, increasing the level of praise will ultimately be as important as the tokens in changing and sustaining the child's behaviour. Praise will also significantly improve the general atmosphere in the house and it becomes a virtuous circle. The more praise given, the happier the child, the more likely he is to behave, and the more praise he will receive.

How Long Should the Tokens Run For?

It is important that this process has a time limit. The token system is to help parents to regain control. When this has happened and the parents feel they have authority again, then the tokens can end. It requires considerable organisation to have the right coins ready every morning, as well as discipline to keep the focus on the target behaviour.

Initially aim to keep going for four weeks. This will allow time for the teenager to go through the initial resistance phase and still have time to consolidate the good behaviour. If you get towards four weeks and the change is not yet settled then allow a couple more weeks. I would not recommend going on for more than eight weeks as an absolute maximum. Ultimately, you want the child to behave not for the money, but for the social and emotional benefits of being a functioning member of a happier and more contained family, where there is less conflict and the parents are in charge. When you begin the token system it is a good idea to explain to your child how long it will be going on for.

Common Concerns with Behaviour Tokens

When I introduce the idea of using tokens parents often come out with a whole range of reasons why they won't work. They have often become so stuck that they can't imagine things getting better and are overwhelmed by what they are having to deal with. Here are some common concerns.

- *My child isn't motivated by money*

  There are very few children who are really not motivated by money. Even if this is the case, the token system will still work because the parents will be more consistent and calm in their responses to the child. The parents will be noticing good behaviour and praising it when they see it. As the process goes on the child will notice that the relationship with his parents has improved and he is getting nagged less and having fewer rows. Contrary to how it may seem, children don't want to be fighting with their parents.

  Children will often pretend not to be motivated by money as a way of sabotaging the plan and testing whether their parents are serious. Saying *'I don't care'* is a powerful defence that children will consistently use. Parents will need to be committed to come though this initial stage, even when it feels as though the plan is not working and there is no change.

- *My child deliberately loses all his tokens every day*

  This is quite common at first. The child is unconsciously looking for ways to test if the parents are being serious or if this is just another new regime that will be history in a few days. By using up all his tokens the child has taken control of the process. If you have no more tokens to take away then you have no more leverage over him. At this stage parents have to stick to their guns. The child has got to feel the consequences of his actions and often a few days of being really broke will focus the mind. If he is hell-bent on blowing everything then he will use the tokens as a way of feeding the conflict. Then you will have to be creative and contrive the situation so he does earn some money. If he doesn't earn anything, then he won't see the benefits of behaving. A good way of doing this is to spend a day apart from each other. If you are both in the house for a whole day or evening, there is lots of time for you to cross swords and he can mess things up. If one of you is out for the day then you reduce his opportunities to blow it and the next morning he will be pleasantly surprised when he gets his money. If he can manage to earn some money for a few days on the trot then he will start to be drawn into the process.

- *I let her get away with it because I can't face the row*
  As parents we can easily get into the habit of ignoring our child's behaviour because if we make a fuss the reaction is so extreme that it isn't worth the explosion that follows. This is exactly why the teenager behaves this way. If she raises the stakes high enough, then she realises that her parents won't be able to face telling her off and she will be left alone. It represents a challenge to the parent. *'Is it really worth it?'* This is contrived teenage behaviour and we must be careful how we handle it. The most important thing is not to get hooked in emotionally and to try and stay calm. When parents

are using the token system, they have to be prepared not to let things go. At other times in the book I mention ignoring teenage behaviour as a way of not getting caught up by it. You can still do this with hard cases, but not with the specific behaviour you are targeting. If she is losing tokens for being rude and she is rude, then you *must* take a token away from her. Be prepared to ride out the explosion and if necessary take off another token if the rudeness continues. Remember only to take tokens off for the target behaviour, not for anything else, and don't get into an argument.

- *He has been really good all day. I don't want to ruin it by being picky about his behaviour.*
  It is easy to respond this way, especially towards the end of the time limit for the tokens. If you do respond like this, the message you send is inconsistent. When you are out of hard-case mode, then you can be more flexible, but while you are using the tokens you have to follow through with the consequence, no matter how harsh it seems. If you start to loosen the reins when your teenager's behaviour gets a bit better then you will soon find things slip right back.

Getting Tara Back on Track: A Case Study

Melissa and Luke were having a nightmare with their 15-year-old daughter, Tara. She had always been the most difficult of their two children and her older sister Penny had gone through adolescence without a hitch. As Tara grew older she seemed to become more and more difficult. She was obsessed with her friends and her life seemed to revolve around meeting, talking to or texting them. The more interested she became in her friends, the less notice she seemed to take of anyone at home. Initially Melissa was pleased that Tara was making friends. She had previously been socially rather awkward and her new mates seemed to be a reasonably sensible lot. At the same time, Luke had to work particularly long hours. He was bidding for a new project and was rarely home in the evenings before nine and at weekends he was either working or catatonic with exhaustion.

Melissa became really concerned about Tara as her GCSEs loomed. At parents' evening her teachers predicted she was going to be lucky to get Cs, despite being a very able girl. The biggest worry for Melissa and Luke, when he was around, was the total lack of communication from Tara. She began to come in at random times of the day or night, hungry, exhausted and sometimes, Melissa was pretty sure, drunk. Though Melissa hadn't actually seen any cigarettes, she could smell them. Having had such an easy ride with Penny, Melissa and Luke were totally unprepared for Tara's anger and aggression when they asked her reasonable questions about her plans or whereabouts. Once when Melissa asked Tara if she could be around for Sunday lunch to see to her grandmother, she turned on her mother and screamed 'Stop trying to fucking control me all the time, I'm not a baby.' She then stormed out of the room in tears and spent the rest of the evening on the computer. When Sunday came, Tara managed to be quite sweet to her grandmother, sitting and chatting to her for half an hour. Then she got an emergency text that necessitated her leaving the house at a moment's notice and disappearing off for the rest of the day.

Melissa persuaded Luke that he was going to have to get involved. He tried to have a fatherly chat with Tara, which ended with him shouting at her and calling her 'slovenly, sluttish, lazy and rude'. Tara took herself off to her room for the rest of the day and Melissa and Luke ended up having an enormous row. He accused her of being too soft on Tara and she told him that if he showed half the interest in his family that he showed in his work then they wouldn't be in the state they were in.

When I became involved, the relationship between Melissa and Luke was very strained. Tara was pretty much out of their control and they had become so afraid of her tantrums and the emotional fallout that they had stopped challenging her. Tara received an allowance every month that was supposed to cover everything, but she was also getting extra handouts either by bullying or charming her parents. On the rare occasions when she was polite and friendly, Melissa became a soft touch for the money Tara supposedly needed for school books, stationery and homework revision clubs.

We sat down and discussed Tara and I asked what behaviour they would most like to change. There was such a global meltdown in their relationship with Tara that they found it very difficult to isolate one area. I had to push them on this, as the only way they were going to be able to make progress with Tara was if they broke the problems down into more manageable components. In the end, they settled on two: improving communication and time-keeping. I asked them to be very explicit about what they meant by this and then I asked them to imagine, in a perfect world, what good communication between Tara and them would be like. Again, this was hard. They were so dragged down by her rudeness and her appalling timekeeping that they couldn't imagine things could ever be better. I explained that managing Melissa and Luke's expectations was the only way Tara was going to be able to start to change. Together we agreed on some targets for Tara.

- *To speak to us in a civilised way.*
- *To ask permission before you go anywhere and to let us know when you are going to be back.*
- *To come back on time.*

We then broke down Tara's monthly allowance into a daily rate. She was getting 60 pounds a month. This meant Tara was going to get two pounds per day, which when divided by 20 would give her 20 units worth 10 pence that she could lose a day. I explained how to use the units and the level of commitment it was going to need from them to make it work. I emphasised that they were going to have to be rigorous about applying the rules and that they should never back away from taking a token from Tara, however much they dreaded her reaction. Nor could they take away tokens for any other bad behaviour outside the three targets. Melissa and Luke agreed to go to the bank and have a ready supply of cash so that Tara would get her reward first thing every morning. Finally, I asked Luke if he could reduce his working hours for the next four weeks in order that Melissa and he could work together and support each other to change Tara's behaviour. He was reluctant to make this commitment, but I explained that if he couldn't then there was a real chance that the whole thing was going to unravel and they wouldn't just be back to square one, but the situation would become even worse. At this stage I felt it was essential that both parents were available to back up each other and share the burden of the inevitable resistance they could expect from Tara. In the end Luke agreed to come home earlier in the evenings and to be more available at weekends.

On a Sunday afternoon, Luke and Melissa sat Tara down and talked through the plan, ready for it to start on Monday morning. When they had finished they gave her a chance to have her say, but she said nothing and sulked. At first I asked them to call me every other night so I could monitor progress at the beginning and give them some moral support. The first three days went well and Tara was much more compliant. She earned all her pocket money and there was generally a much happier atmosphere in the house.

'She actually seems to enjoy following the rules,' Luke said to me on Wednesday evening. I kept encouraging them to use the 6 to 1 ratio with Tara to stay positive.

When we talked again on Friday, things had gone seriously wrong. On Thursday morning Tara had asked if she could go round to a friend's house. Melissa said that was fine, provided she was back by seven. Tara finally got in at ten to eight. Because this was such an improvement on the last few months, Melissa let Tara off without losing a token. When Luke got back in at half past eight he was furious with his wife. He called Tara down from her room and told her that because she hadn't followed the rule, she was to lose a token after all. Tara lost her temper and swore at her parents and left the house. When she crept back in a couple of hours later, neither of them could face telling her that she had lost two more tokens, one for the swearing and one for storming out, so they left her alone. In the morning, Luke left for work before Tara was up and Melissa gave Tara her pocket money, minus only two tokens. On Friday afternoon, Tara kept her phone switched off and come back an hour and a half late from school. Luke was home early and went into reptile mode, shouting at Tara. When she shouted back, Luke told her she would have no pocket money for the rest of the weekend. We needed to have an urgent meeting before everything completely unravelled.

I wrote down a timeline for what had happened, showing how Melissa and Luke had responded to each situation. My aim was for everyone to stay calm and remain in problem-solving mode. Melissa and Luke were able to pin down what had gone wrong and what they could have done differently. I also reminded them how well the first days had gone. When parents are dealing with difficult teenagers, the problems can seem so overwhelming that it is easy to discount positive times. Luke agreed again to get back earlier and Melissa said she was going to be tighter on taking away tokens. I stressed to them the importance of backing up each other and not running away from confrontations with Tara. I also emphasised the importance of staying out of reptile mode, as the more emotional they became with Tara, the less effective the system would be. I also got them to practise what they were going to say to Tara when they took a token away from her. They found this really embarrassing, but they went along with it anyway. Finally we had to address Luke's decision to take away all of Tara's pocket money for the weekend. I said he was going to have to back down and follow the rules they had devised to the letter. This was going to involve a somewhat humiliating climb down for Luke, which he was prepared to accept. Tara was to lose one token for not saying where she was, one for being back late and one for shouting at Luke.

I had a good feeling about Luke and Melissa. They had been able to reflect and take responsibility for their own mistakes over the first few days. Beneath all the strain, they had a strong marriage which was helping them to stay united at a very tricky time.

The next week started quietly as before, but on Thursday Melissa rang me to say Tara had come in 20 minutes late. She had taken a token away and Tara had sworn at her and gone up to her room. For this Melissa had taken off another token. I congratulated her on staying calm and sticking to the rules. As always I ended the phone call by reminding her to give out lots of praise.

That weekend, Tara was awful. I had warned Melissa and Luke that this was likely to happen, because Tara would need to test out whether they were really serious. Tara was going to push them to the limit for a bit to see if she could appeal to their emotions and force her parents to back down. This was made more likely by the faltering, inconsistent start there had been during the first week. On Friday night, Tara had demanded to be allowed to go to a friend's party. When Melissa had asked her who the friend was, Tara mentioned a name she had never heard before. Tara was also vague about the venue. Luke came home from work and after a quick discussion, he and Melissa decided that they would let Tara go out, but she would have to be back by nine o'clock. Tara flew into a rage. 'What is the point of going out if I have to be back at nine? I am going to be a joke if I turn up and tell my friends I am leaving before the party has even begun. You can both fuck off and you can take your fucking tokens with you.'

With that, she flounced out, got her coat and left the house, slamming the door. At 10 o'clock she still wasn't back and Melissa began to get seriously worried. Tara came in at 11 o'clock and tried to sneak upstairs. Luke was furious with her, but he stayed calm and told her they would talk in the morning. Tara lost five tokens for her behaviour that night and she lost another six for being rude over the course of the day. She stomped round the house, huffing and puffing and refusing to interact with anyone in the family. On Sunday morning, Luke told Tara she was going to have lunch with the rest of the family. Tara swore at her parents again and sat at the table sulking throughout the meal. By the end of the day she had lost all but two of her tokens and she spent the evening hiding in her room.

I let Luke and Melissa know how well I thought they had done and that sticking to the plan under extreme provocation was going to make the weekend they had just had less likely to happen in the future. Luke was concerned that Tara was losing the same amount of tokens for the really serious crime of staying out late as she was for being rude or swearing. He suggested that Tara lost a token for every ten minutes she was late. I agreed with him about the different tariffs, but I suggested that she should lose five tokens for being less than an hour late and ten if she was more than an hour. This would stop Tara playing the system by choosing to trade a bit of lateness for the loss of just one token.

For the next two weeks Tara continued to make Melissa and Luke's lives a misery. They needed a lot of encouragement and on at least two occasions they were ready to throw in the towel. I kept praising them and telling them that things would get better. To their enormous credit they kept going, giving Tara her left-over pocket money every morning. Then there was a change. For three days in succession Tara managed to keep all her tokens. Melissa and Luke were delighted, but also worried that this was only a temporary respite. I said it would only be temporary if they allowed it to be. Melissa said Tara had done so well that she had run out of change and was having to write her IOUs. I counselled against this – the way to ingrain the better behaviour was to keep going with the token system for another three weeks and to be meticulous about giving Tara her pocket money every day. Now was the time to consolidate and if the parents didn't keep to their side of the bargain, then they could hardly expect their 15-year-old daughter to keep to hers. One of the difficulties with bad behaviour, like other types of pain, is that when it has gone, we quickly forget how bad it was.

We met for the last time three weeks later. I could see the tension had lifted from Melissa and Luke and they felt they were back in control of Tara again. I recommended that they now stop the reward system, as it had done its job and was a huge amount of work for everyone involved. It is almost impossible to keep it going for longer than a couple of months and there is a danger that it will begin to lose its impact. The rules could and should stay in place, but the pocket money should be paid monthly as it was before. The token system remained an option if Tara's behaviour went badly wrong again in the future, but I felt Luke and Melissa now had enough skill and confidence to stop things deteriorating to that level again. Before I left, they introduced me to Tara, who I hadn't met before. She was, I was glad to see, just your average stroppy, unconfident, grumpy, enthusiastic, delightful teenager.

Hard Cases: A Summary

1 Turning round the behaviour of a hard case requires determination and commitment from the parents and they must be prepared to work together. Single parents will benefit from having a friend or family member they can talk things through with.

2 Don't try and change all the behaviour at once. Choose one or two things to improve and work on them. Set the target with the child. Be very clear about what you want to see and give him the chance to have his say.

3 Make sure you always have enough cash to give him his pocket money in the morning. No IOUs.

4 Don't shy away from taking a token away for fear of a confrontation. This is an inevitable part of the process. When you take away a token, don't make a big deal out of it and try to stay as calm and dispassionate as possible, however cross you are feeling.

5 Expect your teenager to test you to find out whether you are really serious. If you are prepared for this moment, you will be better equipped to ride out the storm. Keep faith in the system and stick to the plan. The success of the strategy will depend on your ability to be tough when you are being tested.

6 Most importantly, keep praising. Praise the effort your teenager is making, keep encouraging him and let him know when he has done the right thing. If your relationship allows, give lots of hugs as well.

section four

troubleshooting guide

9

academic life

The triangular relationship between the teenager, his school and his home is often one of the biggest causes of stress and anxiety during adolescence. Children who were angelic at their primary school, received brilliant reports, worked hard and behaved beautifully, can suddenly go spectacularly off the rails when they get to secondary school. Out of the blue, parents have to start fielding phone calls from irate teachers complaining about their child, when in the past there had been a flow of prizes and certificates. Other children continue with this serene progress throughout their secondary school as they head on towards top grades at A level and university. What are the reasons for this dichotomy that so often takes place in school when children reach their teens?

We live in a world in which success is measured in ever more narrow terms. Getting a job that will provide lots of money in order to be able to afford more expensive houses, cars, holidays and television sets is too often seen as the only worthwhile aspiration. Children are more aware of the overwhelming importance of money, promoted through celebrity magazines and television. There is also far more wealth on display by individual children. Children are now judged by which phone, MP3 player, clothes and laptops they have. In the past there were far fewer things around to compare. The only time I remember being jealous of anything was when my friend Mark had a cooler pencil case than me.

Schools are more acutely judged on their exam results than ever and often they pass this pressure on to their pupils. That is not to say academic success hasn't always been important, but children today are relentlessly tested and they are constantly being measured against their peers. The first year of the sixth form used to be a time for consolidation, as children had a breather between the strain of GCSEs and A levels. Now it has become one of the most pressurised years of all, as university places are based on the results of AS levels. There is a fear of failure that can begin to infect even the brightest teenagers and lead them towards levels of anxiety that begin to have a negative effect on their performance in school. At the other end of the spectrum there are children who simply can't face the rat race and decide to opt out. I think this narrowing of what constitutes a good education has made many schools less tolerant of children's (and particularly boys') behaviour. The sort of horsing around that used to get put down to youthful exuberance and was largely ignored or sorted out with a bit of humour, is now seen as a serious disciplinary issue.

It is also unfortunate that as we put teenagers through these tests that may impact on the direction of their lives, there are so many other distractions on their radars. How can turgid exam revision possibly compete with parties, friends, sex and music?

teenagers who work too much

It is hard for parents to find the balance between over-pressurising and understimulating children. Many teenagers wouldn't get out of bed in the morning if they weren't prodded and it is depressing to see teenage talent being wasted by lack of motivation. On the other hand, the last thing we want is to push and pressurise our children so hard that we lose the excitement of childhood in the ghastly grind of revision and exams. The most important thing is for parents to be realistic. By the time children are in their teens it is fairly clear how intelligent they are. It is damaging for a child to be constantly trying to bridge an impossible gap between their ability and their parents' aspirations. When it comes to judging the capability of your child, it is worth listening to the advice of teachers who have had hundreds of children pass through their care. However, in institutions which place a disproportionate amount of importance on academic success, you will need to monitor your child's state of mind.

It is also essential to listen to and observe your child. If it seems the joy has gone out of him and he is working every hour of the day, then it may be time to get him to step back and take his foot off the gas. Be aware of changes in behaviour and mood that seem beyond the usual emotional lurches that afflict teenagers. If children begin to sacrifice things they enjoy in order to cram in another frantic hour's revision, then there may be a problem developing. Children who are working every moment of the day are unlikely to be productive and their soaring levels of stress will begin to have a negative effect on their ability to succeed in the exam room. Often it is the peer culture in an unexpected manifestation of FOMO that causes this anxiety, a sense that everyone else is working every hour of the day and sailing towards straight As. Parents have to get the message across that although exams are important they are not everything and the worst that can happen is the child will have to re-take or settle for a different university. At the time this can feel like a catastrophe, but in reality it is unlikely to make much difference to the child's life. There is so much importance put on exams that children can misinterpret the messages they receive and can begin to think their parents' love is dependent on how well they do.

How to Deal with Academic Stress

If you think your child is beginning to overdo it then here are some pointers to help you reduce the stress, make revision effective and give him the best chance of doing well in his exams.

- *Be aware of the messages you are sending*
  Parents can put pressure on their children without meaning to. In high-achieving families the culture of success can be all-pervading and even if parents are telling children not to work too hard, there is still an implicit expectation that they will get A

grades. Oldest children often carry a disproportionate amount of their parents' aspirations and they can be particularly sensitive to this pressure. Younger children who have seen their high-flying siblings succeed before them will also be vulnerable, especially if they are not as bright.

- *Avoid talking about the effects of failure*
  Parents often try to frighten teenagers by talking about the terrible consequences of failing their exams. For children who are already stressed these sorts of remarks will fuel the flames of anxiety. However, it can be helpful to talk about what would happen if things did go badly wrong, as all children have this fear at the back of their minds. Knowing that it wouldn't actually be the end of the world and that you would organise re-takes or look for a different course will reassure them that bad results are not the end of the road.

- *Take control of the revision timetable*
  When teenagers have got themselves in a state and are trying to work every moment of the day it may be time for parents to take control. Teenagers don't have the experience to manage these levels of stress and they won't be able to spot the signs that they are overworking. Sit down with your child and explain that doing too much work is counterproductive and may have a negative effect on his grades. Then create a revision timetable that

provides for a reasonable amount of work every day and factor in proper breaks and leisure time. Get him to plan what he is going to do when he is not working and factor in some reward time, or it may be helpful to organise some activities for him. For many children it is a great relief to have an adult taking responsibility when they are in this emotional free-fall and it is worth parents persisting through the initial resistance they may encounter.

- *Feed them*
  Adrenalin-fuelled teenagers who are frantically revising will often lose their appetites and will live on a diet of sweets and chocolate. Insist that your child comes out of his room and eats with the rest of the family. This will allow you to make sure he is eating enough 'brain food' as well as giving you a chance to monitor his state of mind.

- *Exercise*
  Get them out doing something active every day. A bit of fresh air and some exercise will help to reduce stress and clear the mind.

Teenagers Who Work Too Hard: A Summary

1. We live in a highly pressured society where there is huge value placed on material success. This pressure can be transferred on to teenagers who become terrified of academic failure.
2. Working too hard will have a detrimental effect on the capacity to learn.
3. Beware sending subliminal messages that will frighten your child into working harder.
4. If your teenager is working too hard, then you may need to take control of his work schedule.
5. Make sure your teenager takes time to eat, sleep, exercise and socialise.

Teenagers Who Won't Work

Many parents have a constant battle getting their children to do their homework. This is Christine describing her battles with Tilly.

> *'Every evening I dread that moment when I ask my daughter if she has homework. There is a special moan of anguish that she gives when I look meaningfully at her school bag. The thought of spending an hour not doing exactly what she wants to do is unbearable for her and she will do anything, I mean anything, to get out of it. We go through a nightly ritual in which she denies she has any work or she claims the teacher forgot to set it. Then I get out her school diary, if she hasn't lost it, and I try to decipher the scrawled notes she has written. If I can't make any sense of it then she has to ring up a friend and find out what she is supposed to be doing. This battle often lasts longer than the homework would, if only she got down to it. For the next 20 minutes she searches for the right equipment – how many pens and pencils is it possible for a child to lose in a week? Finally I chase her up to her room, get her to sit at her desk and open her books, but when I come in to check on her 10 minutes later she is lying, half asleep, on her bed.'*

Many parents will recognise and sympathise with Christine's story. Let us look briefly at some of the reasons for this aversion that afflicts so many teenagers.

1. Children are often tired after school and having laboured all day the last thing they feel like doing is sitting down to more work.

2. Teachers set homework to consolidate work that has been done in class and as a result it is boring and repetitive.

3. Children do homework alone and away from the positive feedback and encouragement that they get from their teachers at school.

4. There are so many distractions in teenagers' bedrooms including music, mobile phones, the internet, social networking sites and television, that they can't get down to work.

5. Some teachers are lax about setting and marking homework and if teenagers think they can get away without doing the work then they will.

6. Teenagers don't see the long-term link between doing mundane homework and the glittering prizes of academic success. They have far more important things to think about in the short term.

We may feel sympathy for these reasons for avoiding homework, but it is an inevitable part of schooling and with some preparation, parents can make it less of a battleground.

The theory is simple – if your child isn't completing homework adequately and on time then you need to become involved and take some control of the situation.

Here are my rules for getting teenagers to complete homework.

Communicate

Talk to the school, acknowledge there is a problem and offer to go in and discuss it. The more positive and open the lines of communication are between you and the school, the quicker you will make progress. Schools like it when they feel parents are on their side and are prepared to work with them.

Explain

Sit down with your teenager and explain that you and the school are concerned that homework is not being completed. Find out if there are any genuine reasons for the lack of work and if there are, agree a plan to sort them out. Acknowledge that homework can be boring and is often the last thing she feels like doing, but nevertheless it needs to be done. Say that you are going to be on her case for the next few weeks until she is back on track. When she has proved to you that she can complete her homework without your help, then you will leave her in peace. You are giving her responsibility and control over how long you need to intervene for – if she does it on her own you will leave her alone, if she doesn't then she needs you to be in control.

Gather Information

Make sure she is writing down her homework legibly in her school diary every day. If she isn't, then contact the school and ask if the teachers or her tutor could make sure the diary is being kept up. Many schools now send homework by email, or post it on an interactive website. If it is emailed, ask the teacher to copy you in so you know what has been set. If it is published on a website, make sure you know how to access it. Often teenagers will try to keep you in the dark about both the content and the deadline for their homework. They create a fog around the process that is designed to stop you from knowing what is going on. They may also try to tell you that you won't be able to understand what they are supposed to be doing and give vague or evasive explanations. It is important to see through these smokescreens and find out precisely what is expected. Most teachers are very clear about the activity when they set it and it only becomes incomprehensible when it is translated through the prism of your teenager's brain.

Reduce Distractions

Teenagers' bedrooms are often the worst place to do homework. They have all kinds of distractions that can take them away from their work. If her text alert goes off, then your FOMO-afflicted daughter will have to read it and respond and her concentration will go. If an email or an MSN post arrives, then she will need to do something about it. With a click of a mouse teenagers can be on a social networking site, YouTube or any one of a huge range of places away from getting down to work. With all the modern distractions it is remarkable that teenagers manage to get anything done at all. Given how hard it is for teenagers to work in their bedroom, parents then have a choice – either make the room less stimulating or suggest their child works somewhere else. If there is a suitable alternative room in the house where teenagers can work peacefully, then this is an ideal solution. In the case study in Chapter 3, Planning for Better Behaviour, Julia got Marcus to work effectively in her bedroom where there were none of his distractions. He actually chose to continue to work there even after he had won the right to work back in his own room.

If there is nowhere else for your teenager to work then you will have to reduce the distractions in her bedroom. Ideally, parents should involve their child in this process. Ask her to be realistic about what stops her from working and look at what you can do to make homework time more peaceful. If she has a television or a computer in her room then you may have to agree to remove them. You can also ask for her phone or MP3 player while she is doing homework. Parents will often be surprised at how compliant their children are about reducing distractions. Teens often hate that feeling of homework hanging over them and are relieved to get it out of the way.

Another alternative is to look into what is available at school. Often there is a nightly after-school homework club which means that everything is finished before your teenager even gets home, thus taking homework rows out of the equation completely. Many teenagers find it hard to go to homework clubs, there is a FOMO factor created by all their friends going off together whilst they stay behind and work in a classroom. If your child can get over this, then she may accept the pay-off of completing homework at the end of the day in the distraction-free environment of a classroom.

Homework Kit

One of the great time-wasting techniques of teenagers (and the rest of us) is not to have the right equipment. Hours can be spent aimlessly looking for a rubber or a pencil sharpener and teenagers seem to be able to magically vaporise pens and pencils. Have a small box in which you keep a pencil, a pen, a pencil sharpener, a rubber, a ruler, a calculator (never let them use the one on their phone, or they might just have to reply to that text and see who that missed call was from) and, if necessary, compasses and a set square. Have spares available so you can top up when things get lost. Remember, you are helping her to do her homework, not focusing on her organisational skills, so don't try and change more than one thing at a time. If she is not capable of looking after the box, then hang on to it and present her with it at homework time in the evening. When she has finished, you can get her to put everything back.

Timing

Being clear about timing is a useful tool in the process of taking control of your child's homework schedule. Having a set time in the evening when she does her homework will stop her from putting it off until it's time to go to bed.

Earlier in the evening is better, before she has relaxed too much and when there isn't much on television. Also, try and get weekend homework done on Friday night or Saturday morning. She will be in a much better mood if she doesn't have it hanging over her until Sunday night. Make the homework time a specific length, half an hour for younger teens and up to an hour and a half as they get older. Giving a finishing time will help them to build up the self-discipline to complete the work in time and will not make the work seem to stretch out endlessly into the night.

Check Up

Children who are not doing their homework need to be on a tighter rein. We have discussed getting clarity about what the work actually is, so that parents can then check it has been done. Even if GCSE maths is beyond you and you can't make head or tail of your daughter's homework on trigonometry, you can still get a sense of the quality and effort that has gone into it from looking though it. Don't allow them to fob you off with excuses about why it hasn't been completed. Often teenagers will do a chunk of the work, get bored, and say they will finish it in the morning. If you have made the rule that homework needs to be completed every night then stick to it. If you don't, then the message is, *'How much homework you need to do is up for negotiation'*. The result will be a nightly battle about what is acceptable and a brisk return back to square one. Be wary of teenagers saying they don't understand the work. This can often be translated as meaning, *'I can't be bothered to engage enough brainpower to work out what I am supposed to be doing.*' If she genuinely can't do the work and she has given it her best shot, then write a note to the teacher with an explanation. As a parent of a teenager you will be bombarded with a range of highly creative excuses as to why homework doesn't need to or can't be done. If you have clear routines established for doing homework, then you won't be sidetracked into a nightly argument about what needs to be done and when.

Rewards

If your teenager is struggling to get down to homework, you can set up a system that rewards her for completing it. The most simple (and effective) is a little financial incentive. One pound if all the work is finished on time may just give her the extra boost she needs. When, after a few weeks, she is back in the habit of doing the work, you can get off her back, stop giving the reward and allow her to do her homework when she wants. Alternatively, you can link the completion of homework to some of her pocket money or her allowance. Don't allow her to talk you into big rewards or keep the system going for too long. Homework is one of those chores that we all have to do and you don't want her only doing it for the money. Once the pattern and habit of doing homework has changed then you can stop using rewards. Parents often worry that when they stop giving a reward the teenager will slip back to the old habits, so encourage your teenager to give herself a little reward once she has completed her homework.

Sanctions

What if she still doesn't do her work? Plan a sanction that you can use if the work isn't done. This needs to be easy to administer and linked to the work. Such as, *'If you don't complete your homework on time then you can't go out on Saturday.'* Keep the sanction simple and whatever you do, follow through with it. For example, if the rule is *'No homework, no screen time'*, then don't be tempted to back down because you can't face the row if you stick to your guns. If you show weakness, your decisions will be challenged.

Use 6 to 1

Acknowledge that homework can be a real pain at times and praise your teenager for getting it done. She gets feedback from her teachers for her hard work at school, but doing homework is a lonelier business. Let her know you have noticed and appreciated the effort she has made with getting down to work, doing it well and completing it. Remind her to give herself a treat.

Teenagers Who Won't Work: A Summary

1. Homework can be a real drag for teenagers who have all sorts of other things they would rather do. However, it is a reality of teenage life and we can encourage children to develop good homework habits.
2. Communicate with the school.
3. When teenagers are not doing their homework, parents need to take control and make a plan that includes rewards, sanctions and praise.
4. Reduce distractions by removing them from the room or finding a less stimulating place in the house for homework.
5. Get together a homework kit that means your teenager can get straight down to work without fussing about pens and rubbers.
6. Check that the homework has been done.
7. Encourage your child to reward herself when she has completed her homework.

Trouble at School

'When my phone rings and the school's number comes up, I get a feeling of dread in the pit of my stomach. When I answer I am tempted to cut the small talk and just say, "Now what has she done?" Elaine's form tutor has a special sort of caring voice she puts on, that makes me want to slap her. I then listen to a string of complaints about her laziness, her lateness and her rudeness. I apologise and grovel profusely and I say I will have a word with Elaine when she gets back from school. It goes quiet for a couple of weeks and then they are back on the phone.'

Many parents of teenagers will be familiar with this scenario. Some children are fine at home and yet seem to turn into monsters when they go through the school gate, this behaviour can often be associated with failing academically at school. Some are a nightmare at home and yet are perfect at school, never appearing to put a foot wrong. Others seem constantly to be in trouble wherever they are.

Parents can become really frustrated with complaints from school. *'It's their problem,'* a parent once said to me, *'if their teachers are so weak that they can't control the class properly. What am I supposed to do about it at home?'* A breakdown in relations between home and school will start to have a negative effect on the child's education. Parents can begin to feel the school has *'got it in for'* their child and that they have begun to give up on her. Parents dislike it when the school doesn't tell them anything is wrong until things have got really serious. When it turns out that their teenager has been really difficult for weeks, parents feel that some communication earlier on might have helped to nip things in the bud.

These two ends of the spectrum of communication with school – too much or too little – can become a huge source of frustration for parents. What can parents do to improve communication with schools and how can parents and schools work together to give their child the best chance of success?

It is important to consider why teachers get so stressed by bad behaviour in school. At secondary school the main way teachers will be judged on whether they are doing their job properly is by the results of their pupils. Most children, most of the time, are compliant and keen to work. By the time they are teenagers they have had the importance of academic success drummed into them. When there is one individual or a group of children in the class with their own agenda, which appears to be socialising, messing about and avoiding doing work, teachers become extremely frustrated. They can see that the disruption is beginning to affect the work of the other children and they dread the reaction of parents and their head teacher if the class underachieves. Some teachers and schools do not have the skills, knowledge and resources to deal with the most challenging children and after a bit they begin to run out of ideas. When they ring parents up to complain, they are often projecting the frustration they are feeling with the child on to the parents. They want the parents to do something, but they don't always know what. Some of the best and most reasonable teachers can become fixated on the behaviour of one or two individuals and start to believe that without them their job would suddenly become easy.

So what we have is tired, stressed and frustrated teachers ringing up tired, stressed and frustrated parents to dump their feelings about a difficult child. It is no wonder that this can become a source of anger and conflict.

The best schools and teachers will have a plan that they can engage when things start to go wrong. They stay positive about the situation and they anticipate a successful resolution.

How You Can Help to Improve Your Child's Behaviour at School

- *Organise a meeting*
  If you are receiving complaints about your child from school, don't try and deal with them over the phone or by email. Make an appointment with the school and meet the teacher or teachers concerned. The school will appreciate that you are taking their complaints seriously, and you will get a much better sense of the issues and be able to plan solutions if you are sitting face-to-face.

- *Acknowledge the school's point of view and the teacher's feelings*
  Parents may be furious with the school and may think the school is handling the situation appallingly, but nevertheless they have to accept how the teachers are feeling and to take these emotions into account when they communicate with the school.

How to Handle Meetings with the School

For the first part of the meeting you will probably have to sit and listen to a litany of complaints – how he is disorganised, disruptive, a bad influence on others, cheeky, messy and so on. It is horrible to hear your child being talked about like this and it is very hard not to take this personally and see it as a criticism of your parenting. One mother described feeling like a naughty schoolgirl when she was called into school for a meeting. *'They had set the furniture up so that I was almost surrounded by them and they took it in turns to tell me how terrible my daughter was. At the end they didn't offer any solutions or ideas as to how we could make the situation better. I walked out feeling miserable and helpless.'*

This scenario is all too common for many parents when they go into school for meetings. Parents often have grievances of their own and there is a temptation to go in all guns blazing. Unfortunately, this will only put the school on the defensive and all parties will start to go into reptile mode. If parents do have issues they wish to raise, then they should do this calmly and stick to the facts.

Once everyone has had a chance to air their views then there is an opportunity to start to problem solve. The most effective solutions are those in which home and the school are supporting each other and the lines of communication are kept open. This means the teenager is unable to throw up a smoke screen and convince his parents he is the model pupil. If the school gives the parents weekly (or daily in severe cases) feedback then parents can link performance in class to pocket money, or some other simple reward. They can also impose a simple sanction when things go wrong. It is likely the teenager will see this as colluding and ganging up between the adults so it is important, however difficult things are, for parents to continue to praise and find positive things to say to their teenager.

Exclusion

If the situation becomes really dire then the school may begin to mention exclusion. This is less likely to happen if the school sees the parents being supportive. Schools tend to permanently exclude pupils when they feel there is nowhere else to go. If your teenager is reaching this point, it may be useful to agree a reduced timetable for a couple of weeks while everyone has a chance to reboot. If your child has been at risk of being permanently excluded and has made an improvement, ensure you draw this change to the school's attention. Sometimes the bad-boy label can stick for a long time. As a rule, I am not in favour of moving children from school to school, but when relations have got so bad that permanent exclusion is beginning to look inevitable, sometimes it is better for you to jump before you are pushed. Finding another school with the stigma of permanent exclusion attached to your child is tough and makes a fresh start more difficult.

If your child is permanently excluded, the school is obliged to explain the appeals procedure. If you think you have a good case against the exclusion, it is worth fighting to remove the tag of exclusion from your child, even if you have already decided that he will not go back to that school. Other state schools with capacity are obliged to offer your permanently excluded child a place. Unfortunately, arriving with a permanently excluded tag will immediately make the school look out for any signs of challenging behaviour. There is a danger they will be less tolerant than they would be with their own troublesome pupils. The alternatives are sixth-form colleges for older children, private schools, or unbelievably expensive tutorial centres.

As you suffer the trauma and stigma of having a teenager thrown out of school, never lose sight of the importance of maintaining your relationship with your child. Try not to let the anger, disappointment and guilt get in the way of your love. The storm may rage to the exclusion of everything else – but it will pass.

Trouble at School: A Summary

1. Bad behaviour is a threat to schools and teachers. Emotions will often be running high.
2. Arrange to meet face-to-face with the teachers and be supportive and positive even if you are furious with the school.
3. Don't let the meeting turn into a character assassination of your child. Focus on getting positive results and a plan to move things forward.
4. Stay in close communication with the school and monitor your teenager's progress. If he starts doing better make sure the school are registering this and noticing the change.
5. If your child is in real danger of permanent exclusion, then consider moving schools.
6. When things get really bad, don't lose sight of the importance of retaining a positive, loving relationship with your teenager.

10

home life

Teenage Tantrums

Right at the beginning of the book, in Chapter 1, we looked at how a combination of the rewiring and growth of the brain, hormones and the process of separation from parents is the cause of a lot of teenage behaviour. One of the most common and spectacular examples of this is the teenage tantrum. Many parents walk on eggshells around their teenager, fearful that they may unwittingly be the cause of a force-ten tantrum. The most common characteristics of the teenage tantrum are screaming, shouting abuse, storming out of rooms, banging of doors, crying and sulking.

Tantrums are a form of communication. They are a technique for teenagers either to get their own way or to express their anger or frustration. For some teenagers, tantrums work very well. They have learnt that if they ask nicely, they don't always get what they want, but if they really let rip, or even make threats, then parents will give in to keep the peace. This teaches teenagers an unfortunate lesson that they may become stuck with – we can all think of adults who have learnt to throw tantrums when they don't get what they want.

Tantrums may be at times a powerful and effective method of communication, but they are not acceptable as a way of behaving. Here are some ideas for reducing the intensity and frequency of teenage tantrums.

- *Don't avoid necessary confrontations*
  There is a real temptation for parents not to challenge their teenage child because they can't face the tantrum that will follow. Many teenagers are quite comfortable with having a row and losing their temper. This then gives the teenager huge power that they will exploit to get their own way. When confronting a teenager, take into account the three rules of communication – tone, timing and text – but don't shy away from having a conversation because you are worried about the reaction you might get. If you do, you will encourage the behaviour and build a pattern that will become harder to unravel as time goes by.

- *Don't give in*
  However big the explosion, however impressive the amateur dramatics, don't give in to a teenage tantrum. As soon as you do, the message becomes, *'No means no, unless you really push me, in which case no means, oh all right then.'* By all means argue or discuss with a calm and rational teenager, allow

them to put their case – you really might have got the wrong end of the stick, but as soon as they start to act like a diva with a headache, then negotiations are over. Stick to your guns and don't change your mind.

- *Stay calm and don't get pulled in*

Easier said than done, I know, but if you can stay calm and not get hooked into an argument then you will retain your authority. If you start to argue or lose your temper yourself the chances are, in reptile mode, you will end up saying and doing things that will make the situation worse. Teenagers can use tantrums to deflect your attention away from the issue at hand. By drawing their parents into a screaming row, teenagers can conveniently make them forget the original problem. It is useful to have a little script to use when your teenager has lost his temper with you. Stand in a relaxed pose with your palms open in a non-confrontational way and repeat a couple of times, *'When you're calm, we'll talk.'*

If teenagers start to smash things up, then don't try to intervene until they have finished. Make putting everything back together again part of the consequence.

- *Beware pay-offs*

Sometimes teenagers can get a big emotional pay-off from having a tantrum. They can come in afterwards with a guilt-inducing, simpering apology and the parent can be seduced into giving in and letting their child do whatever he wanted to do. Parents are particularly vulnerable to this if they have lost their tempers themselves.

- *Ignore them*

  When teenagers go off in a screaming huff, telling their parents how much they hate them, there is a temptation to either go after them and have a row, or go and check if they are okay and to try and seek some sort of solution. If your teenager has really lost it then there isn't much point in talking to her anyway until the reptile has gone away. As we know from experience, sulking without an audience is a boring and pointless exercise. If you give it an hour or so, your teenager will usually come back without being chased. When teenagers do return to the civilised world after a tantrum, don't go for an over-the-top welcome but simply acknowledge them. Don't get into a protracted prodigal son show as this may also give an emotional pay-off that could make tantrums more likely in the future.

- *Don't let it go*

  When a teenager returns from a tantrum it is all too tempting to carry on as normal and pretend nothing happened, because you are so relieved it is over and you don't want to provoke any dramatic aftershocks. If your teenager has shouted and sworn at you then you need to sort it out. When you are sure he is calm, talk to him about what he did and said and explain that his behaviour is not acceptable. He needs to understand that this is an inappropriate and fruitless way to communicate. If tantrums occur regularly then be prepared to have a sanction such as the loss of a day's pocket money every time it happens. Also praise and reward teenagers when they do stay calm and stay in control of their emotions or show their anger in an appropriate way. *'You must have been really angry, but you dealt with it in the right way.'*

- *Teach them how to be angry*

  Parents who frequently lose their tempers are demonstrating to their children that this is a reasonable way to behave. If teenagers see their parents dealing with arguments or disagreements calmly and rationally they will learn how to solve their own problems in a similar way. Teenagers have to learn that though it is okay to be angry, those feelings have to be managed in an appropriate way. Don't be afraid to talk about their anger and help them to develop some ideas that will enable them to deal with it in a more appropriate way. Encourage them to say if they are angry and to have a plan to follow, so that rather than shouting at their parents they can learn to take some time in their rooms and then come back when they are calm and able to problem solve again. When teenagers are staying calm, or dealing with their anger appropriately, then they can be given a bit of leeway and allowed to get their own way.

The more parents are able to minimise the effect that a teenage tantrum has on them and the more teenagers realise that screaming won't get them anywhere, the fewer of these outbursts they will see.

Tantrums: A Summary

1. Tantrums are a way of communicating. Teenagers use them to release overwhelming emotion that they can't channel. It is up to the parents to decide how effective they are going to allow tantrums to be.
2. Try to stay calm. Avoid sarcasm and don't shout at a teenager who is in the process of storming out. Children learn most from seeing how their parents behave.
3. Never give in to a child who is having a tantrum.
4. If it is becoming a more frequent problem, put a sanction in place for tantrums and use rewards and praise when he is able to stay calm.
5. Teach your child how to be angry in a way that doesn't make things worse.

11

virtual life

Teenagers and Technology

The wide open spaces of the internet provide both opportunities and dangers for teenagers. This chapter will help parents navigate a way through the complicated issues that are raised by computers and mobile phones.

Parents have three major concerns with new technology: the amount of time their children spend on their computers and phones, what they are looking at and who they are communicating with.

Without some parental guidance and control, there are many teenagers who would happily spend their lives disappearing into a virtual twilight world from which they would only emerge to raid the fridge. Teenagers can develop a self-sufficiency with the internet that means their intellectual, social, musical and sexual needs can all be met online. They can lose all touch with genuine human interaction, but for gawky, awkward children who feel uncomfortable in their own skin, this can be a relief. Why go through the pain and embarrassment of talking to real girls when you can reinvent yourself online as a mixture between Superman and George Clooney? The internet can be a mask for the anxieties of growing up and it is no surprise that teenagers find comfort and solace in it. The challenge for parents is to encourage healthy use of the internet that allows children the freedom to explore and enjoy technology, without it taking over their lives. This is made more complicated by the fact that most teenagers will be far more computer savvy than their parents. Nevertheless, if parents have a reasonable amount of computer know-how, then they can protect their children from the dangers of the internet.

How Can Parents Regulate the Internet?

1. *See the computer while it's in use*

   If children are allowed to have a computer in their room with internet access then it will be harder for parents to regulate and monitor computer usage. A computer placed in a public or semi-public place in the home that is shared by the family means parents can keep a closer eye on what is going on. Teenagers will be reluctant to look at inappropriate web content if there is a likelihood that a parent will come wandering past.

2. *Access protection*

   It is easy to set up user profiles with different security settings for adults and their children. Parents can set up protection for their children's profiles that will limit internet content. This can regulate nudity, swearing, violence and games, as well as any key words parents want to proscribe. These settings are controlled from the parent's own password-protected profiles, with administrator rights over their child's profile, meaning parents can look at web browsing history, time spent on the internet and games played. A regular report on children's internet activities can be sent to the parent's profile. This sort of protection is never totally watertight and children can find ways of getting round controls, however by creating a protected profile for your child you are showing that you take their internet safety seriously. For some this may seem very Big Brotherish, but I think it is entirely reasonable to keep an eye on what your child is up to in his virtual life, as you would in the rest of his life. All kinds of other people are monitoring your child's internet use. Your internet service provider logs the activity on your computer and this information is sold to a range of companies to help their marketing and product development. If they know what your child is up to, then shouldn't you?

3. *Computers in rooms*

Older children need some access to a computer for schoolwork and this will become more and more necessary in the future. This then makes a strong case for children having computers in their rooms.

Depending on the age of your child and the level of trust you have, there are a various levels of control that you can exercise. If you have real concerns about what your teenager might be getting up to then you don't have to allow internet access at all. At some inconvenience, he can load any information and data on to a flash stick and transfer it from the family computer to his laptop and back again, if homework needs to be emailed. Alternatively, you can turn off the wi-fi connection when he is supposed to be doing homework. Children will complain that they need the internet to research their work, but this usually isn't the case. After all, we somehow managed to get through our teenage years without Wikipedia. Otherwise, you can set up protected profiles and you can regulate the amount of time that is spent on the internet as well as what is looked at. The computer can be used as leverage or an incentive for your child to do the right thing, for example if he regularly completes his homework on time, then he can earn the right to have a computer in his room. If homework is not being done, or curfews are not being kept to then the computer can be removed until things change. If you are considering removing your child's computer from his room, do so after a warning and make the removal time-limited and the return dependent on seeing an improvement.

Internet Safety

Teenagers need to be made aware of the possible dangers of the internet. Most schools have now developed good training programmes for children on internet safety and many include parents in this process. Settings on social networking sites should be secure so that only approved friends can access your child's profile. Teenagers should never give out addresses or phone numbers and should be aware that the anonymity of the internet means that they can not always be sure who they are really talking to.

Cyberbullying

The internet provides opportunities for teenagers to bully each other and this has become a serious issue for some children. Social networking sites and MSN give opportunities for bullies to post unpleasant comments and these can be picked up by other users and the problem can mushroom very quickly. Girls have been vulnerable to sexual bullying – they are often put under pressure to take revealing photographs of themselves and post them up. There are common incidents of teenagers posting comments about girls – if they won't have sex, they are frigid and if they will, they are slags. Schools are beginning to take cyberbullying more seriously and are doing more to address the problem. Teenagers who don't have the channels to talk about and discuss cyberbullying are the most vulnerable, which is why I believe it is reasonable for parents to monitor their children's virtual lives. The more open the lines of communication are between parents and children, the more likely these issues are to come out into the open. If you do discover cases of cyberbullying, keep a copy of any telephone numbers or email addresses used and be prepared to go to the school or the police if you are seriously concerned.

Mobile Phones

Most teenagers (as well as most of us) are addicted to mobile phones. If we go out of the house without it we feel naked and vulnerable and if, heaven forbid, we leave it somewhere or lose it we are bereft. FOMO makes mobiles even more important to teenagers. They are able to keep their finger on the pulse of their social group at any time of the day and night and they can monitor their status and the extent they are being included, or left out. Unfortunately, mobile phones don't reduce the unquenchable FOMO, they actually feed it and whereas before, once teenagers were at home they didn't have much idea what their friends were up to, now they can track their every movement. I think it is worth making some family rules about mobile phones, for example, no noisy conversations in public parts of the house, and no answering the phone or checking texts at mealtimes. I believe it is essential that families are able to be together without constant interference from the outside world. If Sunday lunch is interrupted by the beep of message alerts followed by some frantic texting, then the unity of the family becomes threatened.

Teenagers are adept at getting parents to pay for top-ups or contracts for their mobile phones. *'If you don't give me some money to top up then I won't be able to contact you if there is a problem'* is the most common line. Teenagers should learn to use and budget for their mobile phones through their allowance or pocket money. A mother I recently met had made a rule that if her daughter didn't have a topped-up phone then she wasn't allowed out. The mother refused to pay and her daughter had to ensure her phone was kept topped up out of her own money. After a couple of occasions in which she had to stay in because she had run out of credit, the daughter soon learnt to allow enough money for her phone and regulate her calls and texts.

Using Mobile Phones for Praise

Parents shouldn't lose sight of the power of mobile phones in praising and thanking children. They are a cringe-free way of saying something positive to your child that can not be discounted or thrown back in your face. When the relationship between teenager and parent is fraught and you can hardly be in the same room without having a fight, texting is a great way of keeping things positive.

Teenagers and Technology: A Summary

1. Parents need to have a reasonable amount of expertise in computers to be able to keep an eye on their teenagers.
2. If teenagers have a computer in their room, make some rules around its use and be prepared to remove it if the rules aren't being followed.
3. Don't allow teenagers unrestricted internet access. It is easy for parents to put controls on to computers that will regulate how much time their children spend on the internet and what they can watch.
4. Make sure your child has a good idea about internet safety and knows what to do if he is being bullied.
5. Make some family rules around mobile phone use and make sure everyone (including parents) stick to them.
6. Use mobile phones for praising and thanking your children.

12

social life

Teenagers' Friends

Friendships and peer groups have great influence in teenagers' development and parents rightly worry about their children ending up with a bad group. It is difficult but necessary to accept that you cannot choose your children's friends for them and it is likely that some of the people they choose to hang around with are going to be fairly unsavoury. Part of the growing up and growing away that happens in the teenage years involves testing different values to the ones their parents have presented. This means teenagers will, at times, be specifically drawn to people their parents don't like. If parents try to micromanage their child's social life they will actively drive them away and take away the teenager's own responsibility and choice in who they become friends with. We can all think of friends or groups of friends that we made as teenagers who, in full FOMO mode we couldn't bear to be away from. Over time, however, we ended up choosing friends with whom we had mutual understanding and affection and moved away from more superficial friendships and groups.

The difficulty for parents is what to do when they feel the people their teenager is hanging around with are an actively bad influence. There is a temptation to step in and ban these relationships but the result will be to make them more alluring, exciting and dangerous. Parents may also simply get it wrong. They only generally see a fairly superficial version of these friends, who may turn out to be safe, loyal and supportive. The more parents can get to know their children's friends, the better their judgement will be. Teenagers can be very resistant to allowing their parents access to their friends because they are worried about being embarrassed. Encourage your teenager to have friends over, even if this means having to share your house with some fairly unattractive characters. Try to be welcoming and friendly at the same time as giving them space and privacy. It is better that your children feel comfortable enough to have their friends in your home, rather than always meeting elsewhere, leaving you with no way of knowing what is going on. Offering to do something for them, like cook them a meal or give them a lift, are ways of spending time with your child's friends. If you can behave a bit less like suspicious parents, then you will see a better side of your children's friends, however appallingly they are dressed. It is also helpful to get to know their parents. You will usually find you all have the same concerns and priorities. If you are in communication with the parents of your child's friends you will be able to keep better tabs on what they are all up to and your teenagers won't be able to play you off against each other.

'Caroline's mother always lets her do it.'

'Okay, I'll give her a ring and check.'

If left to their own devices many teenagers will while away the time doing nothing with their friends, or eventually finding ways to make mischief. If you feel your child is getting into this pattern then start organising things for him to do. He will be resistant and you will have to get past an innate lack of enthusiasm for anything you suggest, but if you can find a productive activity that he gets into, then he will be able to socialise in a more creative and positive way. There are all sorts of activities that teenagers can get involved with in the evenings or after school, including sports, exercise classes, rock-climbing, swimming, music, art, drama, film-making and charity work. Often, because of FOMO, they are reluctant to do these things on their own, but if you can get their friends involved as well, the resistance disappears.

If you feel your child has got in with a crowd who are having a generally corrosive effect on him, such as encouraging him to skip school or go shoplifting, then it is reasonable to address the issue. In the most extreme circumstances you will have to simply ban all contact. You are the parent and one of your jobs is to stop your teenager making mistakes that could affect his later life. This should not be taken lightly and you should be very explicit about why you have chosen to do it. You may need to take back some control and tighten up on curfews and reduce the amount of independence you allow. If the problem is associated with children at the same school, then arrange to go in and discuss your concerns with staff. If you have banned contact with a person or group, let them know the reasons and ask them to help you to monitor the situation. Your child will inevitably be furious with you for sticking your nose into his social life, but he will deep down appreciate that you care enough to do something.

Bullying

Teenage bullying is often complicated and hard to sort out. Teenagers often feel scared and insecure and one of the ways they can manage this is to affirm social group membership by finding a common enemy to bully. After all, if it's someone else, at least it isn't me. Children on the periphery of a group can also be the victim of bullying. This can often be subtle and involve temporary exclusion from the group. The victim might be welcomed back in, only to be rejected again at a later date. Rather than walk away from this situation, teenagers can actually be drawn into it. The more they feel rejected, the more they want to be accepted and the harder they try. Individual members of the group can actually be good friends with the victim when no one else is around, but when the group is together they are dropped again. This sort of bullying can go on for a long time, and sometimes both the victim and the bullies can fail to recognise it as such.

Parents who communicate well with their children are in a better position to discuss this type of situation and devise some coping strategies. It may be useful to talk about your concerns with your child's school or with the other parents in the social group, so that the situation can be closely monitored. Once the subject is out in the open, your child may decide not to hang around with the group any more and start looking for new friends. The alternative is that they are able to become more assertive about addressing the bullying when it is happening and letting the rest of the social group know that they don't like what is going on. It is important that parents don't get too involved in their child's social world. Only intervene when the problem is frequent and intense. Try not to get too worried about teenage bickering and rows between friends. Part of the growing-up process involves learning to manage these sorts of situations without adult help, but if things are serious then don't be afraid to take action.

Teenagers' Friends: A Summary

1. It is healthy and normal for your teenager to choose friends you don't approve of.
2. Try to get to know your children's friends.
3. Encourage your teenager to have friends round to your house.
4. Only ban contact with friends in the most extreme circumstances.
5. Keep an eye out for social bullying and if you detect it then be proactive about contacting the school and other parents. Help your child to be assertive with his friends.

Drugs, Smoking and Alcohol

Parents have more fear about their teenager getting into drugs than almost anything else. In this chapter I will help parents to understand about the risks, how to spot the effects and what to do if a problem develops. I will also outline how parents can address the issue of drugs with their children and what they can say and do to stop, reduce or make drug taking safer. I will then go on to discuss tobacco and alcohol.

It is a fact that if you know the right people you can have drugs delivered to your door from anywhere in Britain in less time that it would take for an ambulance to arrive. Drugs are ubiquitous from the inner city to the leafy suburb to the remotest parts of the countryside. If you think you live in an area where they aren't any around, then think again. It is highly likely that at some stage during the teenage years your child will be in the presence of people who have taken drugs and the chances are he will be offered some. You won't be able to control his response at this moment, all you can do is hope that he draws on what you have taught him and make a safe choice.

This feeling of helplessness is one of the hardest parts of parenting a teenager. You know what is sensible, he knows what is sensible, but will he be sensible?

The good news is that most teenagers don't actually take drugs and those that do almost always come out of the experience or period of experimentation unscathed. The majority of drugs that teenagers are exposed to are not particularly harmful though there is a risk associated with all drugs. Exposure to harder, addictive more dangerous drugs is becoming more common, but is still fairly rare.

Drugs

Marijuana

Marijuana (also known as pot) is the most common illegal drug used by teenagers. It comes in two forms – either as hash, a black or brown resin with the texture of dried Plasticine or, most commonly, as grass or weed, tightly packed buds of brown-green leaves, stalks and little oval shaped seeds.

Marijuana is usually taken by being rolled into a spliff or joint with tobacco and smoked, though it can be put into a pipe or eaten. The effects are a general feeling of muzzy-headed, relaxed goodwill that lasts for a few hours. It can also cause hysterical laughter and powerful waves of pleasure. People high on marijuana often develop cravings for food and 'the munchies'. Frequent trips to the fridge or the shops for ice cream, sweets and pizza are often a sign that someone has been using the drug.

Dangers, Risks and Side Effects

Many people smoke marijuana for many years with few noticeable long-term side effects. It is, by and large, safer than alcohol, but it is by no means risk-free. Marijuana is not physically addictive like tobacco or heroin, but it can become a hard-to-resist habit for frequent users, for whom being stoned becomes the norm. Once stuck in this pattern it can become difficult for users to wean themselves away from the drug and to experience life without being in a permanent haze.

Marijuana is usually smoked with tobacco and frequent smoking can lead to nicotine addiction. Marijuana smokers used to suggest that there was something pure, natural and healthy about smoking marijuana, but this is nonsense as it has at least as many potentially cancer-causing chemicals as tobacco and long-term users run similar risks to cigarette smokers.

There is also a clear link between psychosis and schizophrenia and marijuana use. It is not certain whether taking the drug actually causes these conditions or whether it acts as a trigger for people who already have a predisposition, but for a few unlucky users, dabbling in marijuana can have profound, life-changing effects. There is also evidence that using marijuana affects the short-term memory, a particular concern for teenagers who are preparing for exams. Marijuana can also be associated with increased paranoia and can be the cause of panic attacks.

Skunk

In the last ten years dealers and growers have produced a marijuana hybrid with far greater potency, called skunk. Skunk has more powerful effects that are longer lasting and deeper and can even cause mild hallucinations. It is like suddenly moving from beer to vodka.

Is Marijuana a Gateway Drug?

Parents are often concerned that smoking marijuana will lead into experimentation with stronger, more dangerous drugs, such as cocaine or heroin. It is true that most heroin addicts were once marijuana users, but the vast majority of pot smokers do not go on to harder drugs.

What are the Signs of Marijuana Use?

Marijuana gives off a distinctive herbal, sweet, slightly oily smell. Like tobacco, it clings to clothes and is quite noticeable. Stoned teenagers will have a slightly glassy look to their eyes, which can be off-focus and reddened. They will seem distracted, vague and somewhat detached (what's new?), and they will make frequent, obsessional sorties to the fridge. They will happily sit for long periods of time in front of the most banal television programmes and will be unmotivated to do anything. It can be difficult to spot if your teenager is stoned, because unstoned teenagers operate in a pretty similar way, but if they are dozier, detached and more tuned out than normal, then they may well have been having a smoke.

The Legal Status of Marijuana

There has been considerable confusion about this in recent years and some young people seem to have convinced themselves that marijuana is legal. This is emphatically not the case. Marijuana was reduced from a class B to a class C drug for a couple of years, but because of fears of the effects of skunk it has reverted to class B again. If police find small quantities or catch teenagers smoking a joint they may give a warning, a caution (that will stay on their record) or possibly arrest them. Any suggestion that teenagers are selling drugs is a much more serious offence and can potentially lead to a custodial sentence. Parents should also be aware that if they allow marijuana, or any other drugs, to be taken on their premises, they are committing a criminal offence.

I have focused on marijuana because it remains the most common drug that teenagers use, but nowadays there is a range of illegal drugs that are more readily available and to which your teenager may be exposed.

Cocaine and Speed

These drugs are stimulants that create a feeling of goodwill and up-beat excitement. Speed (or sulphate) is cheap and the price of cocaine has fallen a lot in recent years. Cocaine is categorised as a class A drug and speed is class B. Both usually take the form of a white powder that is inhaled through a rolled-up bank note or a straw into the back of the nose, where the prevalence of blood vessels near the surface of the skin means it enters the bloodstream quickly. Both drugs increase the heart rate and temporarily reduce the need for sleep. Both drugs induce a pleasant state in which the senses seem heightened and users feel more socially confident.

Dangers include potential damage to the cardio-vascular system by overloading the heart, paranoia and anxiety and accidents caused by lack of sleep. These drugs are cut (mixed) by the dealer with other substances to pad out the drug and make each batch go further. Only a small proportion of pure cocaine will actually be present. Anything from glucose to rat poison can be used to cut speed or cocaine and users have no idea what they are ingesting. As the drug wears off, in a matter of minutes with cocaine or in a few hours with speed, the user experiences a 'low' that can produce feelings of despair and depression. Users begin to 'chase the high', but there is a law of diminishing returns at play here as the body develops tolerance to the drug, and to get the same effect users will need to take larger quantities, thus exposing themselves to a greater level of risk.

Mind-altering Drugs

The most likely drug in this category that teenagers will be exposed to is Ecstasy or 'E'. This drug, created in a laboratory, came to prominence in the late 1980s as part of the rave music scene. It is a 'good time' drug that gives users a feeling of goodwill and love towards their fellow humans. People on Ecstasy can be over-friendly and have the stamina and desire to dance for hours but often wear somewhat grotesque facial expressions as though they are trying to chew a large mouthful of air. Many users chew gum to counter this effect. Ecstasy is a 'going out' drug and is often taken at nightclubs or parties.

The dangers were initially misunderstood and it is now not seen to be as harmful as it was. Users become very thirsty and can find it hard to regulate their water intake. On rare occasions individuals have become ill from drinking too much water. There may be some links between long-term use and depression, but this is as yet unproven. The other drug in this category is LSD or acid. This is much more mind-altering than Ecstasy. Its use is accompanied by hysterical laughter and even hallucinations. These 'trips' can be exciting, stimulating and fascinating, but a bad trip can cause panic attacks, paranoia and even psychosis.

Depressants

Drugs in this category are associated with a sort of mental opting-out. They include heroin, barbiturates and codeine. They make the user tune out of daily life and enter a detached, trance-like state. These drugs are usually smoked by putting them on to tin foil and heating them from underneath with a cigarette lighter. The smoke that comes off is then inhaled. More serious users inject heroin which makes it go further and produces a more intense high. Frequent users of heroin can become physically addicted and face severe potential health and social problems. Thankfully, very few teenagers take heroin.

Legal Highs

There are an increasing amount of so-called legal highs available through the internet. These are drugs that have some sort of pleasurable effect, usually similar to cocaine or ecstasy. Teenagers can easily be convinced into thinking that because they haven't yet been made illegal they are not harmful. The reality is that no one really knows the risks and teenagers have to be wary about being guinea pigs.

How Do I Stop My Teenager from Taking Drugs?

FOMO and peer pressure play a large part in a teenager's decision to sample drugs. By taking drugs children can show affinity with a social group and gain acceptance and affirmation from people they want to get in or stay in with. Taking drugs can also be fun. Not only is there the excitement that comes from breaking the rules, but for the most part the effects of drugs can be pleasurable. Drugs can also help teenagers to escape from the pressure of homework and exams. So how do you encourage your child to steer clear?

There are likely to be moments when your teenager is going to be offered drugs. You can't track his every movement or keep tabs on what he's up to every moment of the day. Being a teenager means becoming more independent and doing things away from the guidance and protection of parents. What are the factors that are going to make your child more likely to say *'No'* at these critical moments?

- *Educate*

  The more your child knows about drugs the more likely he is to make a sensible, informed choice. If he already knows the potential risks then he won't get his drugs education from people who are encouraging him to take drugs. Then, if he does then decide to experiment with marijuana, at least he has a better idea of what could go wrong. Education will help him to discern between the most and least dangerous drugs, as well as deciding whether or not to try drugs in the first place. Many schools now operate a sensible drugs education programme in which there is a realistic discussion around drugs, their effects and the risks, rather than the sort of sensational drugs lectures that used to try, unsuccessfully, to frighten children into abstinence by exaggerating the risks. Parents can follow this lead. If you feel ignorant about drugs then look for more information and be open with your children about discussing drugs.

- *Make your message clear*

  Decide on what message you want to give about drugs, and stick to it. Your children need to know what your values and opinions are. These give your children a benchmark to work from, even if they choose to ignore it. I would suggest making it clear to your children that you don't approve of drug taking because of the health risks associated with it, the effects it may have on schoolwork and the fact that they are illegal. On the other hand, be sure they know your disapproval is on a sliding scale and that there are some drugs you would be much more worried about than others. Remember that if you make a big deal out of drugs and tell your children never to take them, there is a danger of giving them perverse encouragement.

- *Not in the house*
  Don't ever allow your teenagers to take drugs under your roof. Some parents feel they would rather have the problem close to home where they can keep an eye on it, but there are all kinds of legal and social risks associated with allowing lawbreaking to go on under your roof. By providing a safe haven for your child to take drugs, you are potentially providing a haven for all his friends as well and by tolerating drug use you are effectively condoning it. Also, how far does your tolerance go? You might allow a bit of pot smoking, but what happens if children come round to your house to take Ecstasy?

What Do I Do if I Suspect My Child is Taking Drugs?

First of all, stay calm. The realisation for parents that their child is experimenting with drugs can be a terrifying shock and it is easy to fly off the handle and overreact or behave in a way that makes drug-taking more, not less, likely in the future. Take some time to weigh up your evidence and if possible talk your response through with your partner. There may be a temptation to wade in with furious, finger-wagging bollocking, but this may alienate your teenager and cause him to clam up.

When you are calm and out of reptile mode, sit down with your teenager and talk through your concerns. If you have found direct evidence, either the drug itself or drugs paraphernalia such as cigarette papers, then show him. Ask him for his opinions and views. However you feel about what he says, try to accept it without making judgemental remarks. The more the conversation operates like a dialogue, the better the chances of a satisfactory outcome. When he has had a chance to put his side of the story, explain your views on the matter. Talk through the risks of drug-taking and the effects it could have on his schoolwork and his future. You can also say what you are worried about as a parent and how you need to be able to trust him when he is out and about. Tell him that if he is taking drugs when you let him out at the weekend or in the evenings then you are going to have to take more control over his time and restrict his freedom. If you feel it is necessary then you can introduce a tighter curfew for a time, but it will probably be a good idea to give him a warning first. If you make too big a deal out of it and give out a harsh punishment, you will probably cause so much resentment that he won't learn from it.

If your child is consistently taking drugs and this is beginning to affect his schooling, then it may be necessary to tighten things up for a period of time (See Chapter 8: Hard Cases). Remember you are the adult and ultimately you can take control if you need to. A bit of dabbling in drugs is common among teenagers and is unlikely to be a big problem, but if the frequency and intensity of drug-taking increases, then a more serious situation can develop. Be prepared to ask for help if you are worried. Your GP should be your first port of call but the National Drugs Helpline also offers advice both for users and for their friends and families.

Smoking

If you smoke, then your children are far more likely to smoke. Therefore, the best way to stop your children from smoking is to give up yourself.

Like drugs, the key to avoiding smoking is a knowledge and understanding of the risks. It is very hard for children to associate what they do now with serious health problems unimaginably far into the future. For many teenagers, the short-term gain in kudos among their friends easily outweighs the distant possibility of lung cancer or heart trouble. However, some teenagers are able to understand the risks and will often choose not to smoke because of them.

You can use other more immediate forms of leverage to put teenagers off smoking, for example how the smell of smoke on their clothes and breath will put off friends of the opposite sex. You can also talk about the cost. Smoking a modest ten cigarettes a day adds up to over 1000 pounds a year. Think of all the other things this money could buy! Keep the discussions low key and calm. If you are too heavy-handed then it is possible that you can make smoking seem exciting and rebellious.

As with drug-taking, I would not allow my teenagers to smoke in the house. The rest of the family's health should not be compromised to keep teenagers happy. You may decide that if their friends need to smoke then they can do it in the garden, but make sure all cigarette butts are picked up.

If your child starts smoking, try to stay calm and

discuss it with him. Allow him to have his say, but be insistent about the risks and how you can not condone it. By coming down too heavily on a smoking teenager there is a danger that they will just get better at hiding it. Give him a book about how to give up, such as Allen Carr's *Easy Way to Stop Smoking*. The sooner they are able to give up, the easier it is to stop and the less damage is done to their lungs. If your teenager becomes a serious smoker you can try to take control by enforcing strict curfews and restricting pocket money, but this probably won't help him to choose to give up. Without condoning smoking you may have to accept that it is happening and simply be available to help when he chooses to give up.

Alcohol

I believe alcohol is a bigger problem for teenagers than either smoking or drugs. Drugs are relatively rare and most of them aren't particularly harmful. Cigarettes do not have social problems attached to them and most teenagers are sensible enough to give up after dipping their toe in the water for a bit. Even if they don't straight away, they have plenty of time to do so before their health starts to become seriously affected.

Alcohol, on the other hand, causes short-and-long term health problems and can also be the cause of serious social problems for teenagers. There has been a huge increase in the amount of alcohol consumed by teenagers in the last 20 years and there has been a ten-fold increase in teenagers being admitted to hospital under the influence of alcohol. Some drinks that are marketed for young adults taste sweet and refreshing, but contain high levels of alcohol, so teenagers get drunk without realising it is happening. Teenagers are often not aware of the pitfalls of drinking. Alcohol can make them belligerent and they can get into arguments or fights. Girls lose their inhibitions and are far more likely to have sex when they are drunk. They are also less likely to insist that their partner uses a condom and so there is increased risk of pregnancy and sexually transmitted infections. Teenagers are vulnerable to the physical effects of drinking too much, such as passing out in a public place, having accidents, choking on their vomit or developing heart or liver complaints. There is also a trend for taking photographs of drunk people and then publishing them on the internet.

How Do I Stop my Teenager Drinking Too Much?

As with smoking, parents' attitude to drinking is important. If children are brought up in a house in which there is a lot of drinking, where people are seen to get drunk and complain about the effects of hangovers, then children will see this sort of behaviour as acceptable. I am not for a moment suggesting that parents don't drink in front of their children, but it is important for teenagers to see parents using alcohol in moderation and not as an emotional crutch. I believe parents should introduce children to alcohol as young teenagers in a sociable, controlled way, for example offering a small glass of cider or a watered-down glass of wine at Sunday lunch. This may help children to avoid experimenting with binge drinking. As they get older, then you can allow them more. Ideally you want them to be able to cope sensibly with the free access to drinking they will have when they go to college or university. It is unfortunate that we Northern Europeans have a culture of getting drunk for the sake of it. As much as possible, children should be shown an alternative way of using alcohol.

It is inevitable that your teenager will get drunk at some stage to find out what it's like. This should not be an excuse for an *'I told you so'* lecture. If the incident is particularly serious then you can amend curfew arrangements, but generally what you want is for your child to learn from his mistake, not be punished for it. If you think your child is going to parties or friends' houses where the rules on alcohol are much more lax than your own then be prepared to restrict your child's freedom, but remember the best outcome is that your child finds his own comfortable, safe, drinking levels himself, that he can carry through to adult life. If you are worried your teenager is drinking too much or is showing some signs of dependence on alcohol, then seek help through your GP or through the Drinkline national helpline.

Parents can feel like a lone buttress holding back the tide of social pressure to indulge in drugs, smoking and alcohol. Parents need to gain a good knowledge of the issues and clearly communicate their values, beliefs and views around the use of these substances, but also be supportive and understanding if and when the child makes mistakes. If the child has a good understanding of the risks, his parents' opinions and an idea what to do if he is worried or things feel they are getting out of hand, then at those crucial decision-making moments he will be more likely to make the right choices. As parents there is no more we can do.

Drugs, Smoking and Alcohol: A Summary

1. It is likely that your teenager will be exposed to drugs.
2. Some drugs are relatively harmless, some are very dangerous. The more knowledge parents have about drugs, the better they can respond if their child begins to experiment.
3. The better-educated teenagers are, the more likely they are to make sensible, safe choices when it comes to drug-taking, smoking and drinking.
4. Smoking is an understandable worry for many parents, but at least teenagers have plenty of time to see sense and give up before they do themselves any lasting damage.
5. Alcohol often poses a greater risk than drugs.
6. Teenagers should be taught sensible drinking habits. Parents should be careful about how they drink in front of their children.

Sex

From an early age, children are exposed to images of sex. Soap operas show people kissing passionately before cutting to a scene of post-coital bliss in which the characters discuss how they are going to stop his wife from finding out.

Sex is used as a subtle and a not-so-subtle tool to sell anything, from luggage to confectionary *'buy this car and you will get to have sex with this beautiful woman'*.

Fifteen-rated films that can be easily rented by 12-year-olds often contain 'strong sex'. This may be tempered by a bit of soft focus and gentle music, but little is left to the imagination and most early teens will know exactly what two people having sex looks like.

In Britain, our teenagers have the highest rates of pregnancy and sexually transmitted infections (STI) in Western Europe and a third of girls under the age of 16 have had sex. Fifteen years ago, the limit of easily accessible pornography was a naked girl draped across a chaise longue in the centrefold of a magazine. The internet now provides a source of free, graphic pornography of staggering range in which every possible sexual peccadillo is catered for. Parents who are not fully aware of the extent of internet porn should put the words 'free sex video' into their search engine and see the astonishing volume of sex that can be viewed with a click of the mouse. A very high proportion of teenage boys and many teenage girls will have seen internet pornography and there is a danger that these images can become their template for how people have sex.

Do you want your child to believe the following?

1. Women are available for sex the whole time.

2. Foreplay is unnecessary.

3. Women have earth-shattering orgasms every time they have sex.

4. All women have voluptuous, curvaceous, perfect figures.

5. All men have enormous penises and marathon staying-power.

6. There is no emotional component to sex.

7. Sex ends when the male ejaculates and he is then free to get up and go.

8. Unprotected sex does not cause pregnancy or STIs.

These are the clear, unambiguous messages that are projected by pornography. You may feel you have excellent safety settings on your computer that protect your child, but you can't be sure what he is accessing at his friends' houses.

During puberty, teenagers' bodies are adapting to make them ready to have sex. They are bombarded with images of people having sex, many of their friends have begun to have sex and peer pressure to have sex grows as they get older. What can parents do to help their children to get through this onslaught safely and relatively unscathed?

I don't believe that *nothing* is an option any more. The days when parents would hope that someone else would do the job for them have gone. It is not sufficient to leave a book about the facts of life lying around in the hope that your teenager will read it and learn all he needs to know without needing to have an embarrassing conversation. Everyone else is talking to our children about sex, so we had better start talking too.

We Need to Talk About Sex

We British are a strange mixture when it comes to sex. On one hand, we have pretty liberal views and there is a lot of sexual promiscuity among young people. On the other hand, we have an *'Oooh Matron'* sense of humour which means we don't find it easy to talk frankly about sex. I am not for a moment suggesting we ban cultural icons like *Carry On* films and birthday cards loaded with innuendo, but I do think we need to be aware of how this attitude can stop us from being as open as we are going to need to be to keep our teenagers safe.

How then should we broach this difficult and embarrassing subject with teenagers? The most important thing parents can do before they talk about sex with their children, is to talk about it with each other. As always, it is helpful for parents to plan in advance. You won't be able to have a set text to follow around every issue of teenage sexuality, but drawing up a template of your own views and values will help you to decide what messages you want to give your children about sex. Your views will almost certainly change and your attitude to questions of sex will depend on the maturity, the gender and the age of your children. However, it is likely you can predict the sorts of issues that are likely to crop up and if you have your response partly prepared you will remain authoritative and measured. What, for example, will you say when your 15-year-old daughter asks if her boyfriend can stay the night in her room?

I think it is essential that parents agree on how they are going to talk to their children about sex and what values they want to transmit to their children. You do not want a situation in which two parents are sending radically different messages to an already confused child. Nor do you want to get caught on the hop by a request from your child and end up making a rushed decision that you come to regret. All too often parents blunder into discussions about sex without knowing what their views really are.

Here are some questions that I think parents should think about and discuss before they talk to their children about sex. For many there will not be clear, unambiguous answers, but by discussing them first, parents will begin to solidify their views.

1. At what age should you begin discussing sex with your children?

2. What is an appropriate age for teenagers to start having sex?

3. Do you have the same attitudes to your daughter's sexuality as you do to your son's? If you don't, how will you justify this to your children?

4. At what age would you allow boyfriends or girlfriends to share a bedroom with your son or daughter?

5. What is your view on promiscuity? Is it okay to have sex with anyone you want as long as you are both consenting adults and no one gets hurt? Or are there dangers associated with this attitude?

6. Is it true that it is better to have sex in a mutually loving relationship?

7. Where does love fit in with sex?

8. To what extent are you prepared to discuss your own former and current sex life with your teenagers? If you did things you regret, is it appropriate to share these experiences with your children?

9. Are you prepared to discuss masturbation with your children?

10. Would you buy condoms for your children?

By discussing these and other questions, parents can fine-tune their own opinions and values, and should have a scaffold for talking about sex with their teenagers. Some parents may be reluctant to discuss their moral values, not wishing to impose their views on their children. However, I believe that children want to know what their parents think. Even if they don't appear to listen or take any notice, they have at least got a framework they can measure their own values and attitudes by. Parents are happy to discuss their moral position on most matters with their children, why not do this with sex? If children choose to ignore their parents' views, it is important not to judge heavily and punish. All children will make some silly mistakes, and some will make terrible mistakes, at these moments parents need to be there to pick up the pieces and help their child to recover.

What Is the Right Age to Talk about Sex?

This is a subject that gets people very hot under the collar. There is a belief that if we talk about sex with children we are in danger of encouraging them to do it. If handled badly, this is a distinct possibility. While I understand the fear that many parents and commentators have about children growing up too fast and being robbed of their childhoods, I am convinced that parents need to educate their children about sex and that this needs to happen before they become sexually active. Retrospective sex education is a waste of time. The amount of detail you give children depends on their age and maturity, but I think by the time they are eight or nine they should know where babies come from and, in a rudimentary way, how they are conceived. By this age children will already be asking questions and it is not helpful to fob them off with stories about storks or planting baby seeds in the garden. There will already be chatter in most playgrounds about sex at this age so parents need to stay ahead of the game. On average, girls are beginning their periods at an earlier age than a generation ago. By the time children are in their teens, I think they should have a good understanding of the physical mechanics of sex and parents should also be communicating their beliefs and values around sex. Armed with this knowledge, young teenagers will be in a position to make sensible decisions about sex when it becomes an issue for them.

How and When to Talk About Sex

I'm not convinced that one big, set-piece sex talk is the best way forward. This might be the easiest way to do it for parents, as they only have to get over their embarrassment once and can then stop thinking about it, knowing they have done their bit. The problem is if the parent and child are both red with embarrassment and wishing the whole thing was over then the conversation becomes rushed and the child won't be able to take much in. There is also a danger that once the talk is finished then discussion of sex is put back on the taboo shelf and children will feel unable to raise issues or ask for guidance when they have questions. There is a temptation to wait for the perfect moment to talk about sex, but unfortunately it may never come so you will have to find a reasonably appropriate time, take a deep breath and get on with it. It helps to think in advance about what you want your child to get out of the conversation and to have an idea how you are going to react to his or her questions. The first time you talk about sex is likely to be the hardest, but many parents are surprised, once the embarrassment is overcome, how much teenagers want to talk about sex with them.

Little and often is the secret. I favour a gradual approach in which sex is talked about whenever it crops up or seems appropriate. Newspapers can lead to fruitful discussions about contraception, the age children should start having sex, STIs and so on. For example, *'It says here we have the highest rates of teenage pregnancy in Europe, why do you think that is?'* Once parents and children have got used to talking about sex without feeling the need to put a paper bag over their heads they will find the conversation flows more easily. The more matter-of-fact you are about sex the less it becomes a big deal and the less you will both end up cringing.

Try not to sound judgemental. You will simply put up barriers, but equally, don't be afraid of saying what your values and beliefs are, while acknowledging the world your teenager is living in. *'I think teenagers are under a lot of pressure to have sex at an early age these days, for the boys it is something they think they can boast about and some girls think having sex will help them to get a boyfriend or become popular. I don't think anybody should feel pressured into doing something as important as having sex,'* sounds much better than, *'It's disgusting the way teenagers behave these days, like rabbits. Well, it's no surprise they end up pregnant or diseased. You're an idiot if you go around behaving like that.'*

It is also useful to ask your children what their views are. You may find they think very similarly to you, or there might be some things that shock or surprise you. The better your lines of communication about sex, the more you will be able to add your voice to all the others relentlessly sending messages about sex to your child. Try to keep discussions around sex low-key and matter-of-fact. If you make too big a deal out of it then you are selling the idea of sex as something illicit and exciting that must be tried as soon as possible.

If you are finding your child has gone off the rails sexually and is being promiscuous and dangerous, then the most important message you must emphasise is safety. This takes two forms – safety from pregnancy and STIs and emotional safety. In the first case the message needs to be about practical advice on using condoms and perhaps the Pill. A surprisingly large amount of teenagers have very muddled ideas about pregnancy (for example, you can't get pregnant if you do it standing up), and these myths need to be challenged. STIs now include serious life-threatening diseases such as HIV and hepatitis and are no longer the cause of a bit of sniggering and a trip to the VD clinic for a dose of antibiotics. Young heterosexuals are the group now most likely to catch HIV and the days when it was associated with gay men and drug abusers are emphatically over. Many teenagers don't realise the seriousness of HIV and, though it can now be treated, contracting the disease is life-changing. Depending on the age of the child, parents may want to take back control and tighten the reins (see Chapter 8: Hard Cases). If this does not seem appropriate then keep emphasising the message about safe sex. *'I am really worried about the way you are behaving because I think you could be putting yourself at risk.'*

Keeping emotionally safe is a harder thing to teach your child. Part of being a teenager is learning to cope with having your heart broken. Teenagers get themselves into confused, negative patterns of behaviour that they don't always know how to break. Good listening and support from parents can be a lifeline. Teenagers may give the impression that they don't give a damn what their parents think and much of what parents say appears to be ignored and rejected, but these rejections should not stop parents from trying. Superficially, parents may feel they are getting nowhere, but on a deeper level the messages will go in. By not giving up, parents are showing that they have not stopped caring or loving.

Sex: A Summary

1. Your teenager is bombarded with sexual images in a way that our generation never was. The sex education you had is unlikely to be enough for teenagers today.
2. Parents should decide what their values, beliefs and their answers to common questions are, so they have answers ready for when they are going to address sex with their children.
3. If you don't communicate your values around sex to your child then you are missing your chance. Everyone else is sharing their views with them.
4. An open, on-going dialogue about sex is better than a one-off birds and the bees cringe-session. Keep it low key and matter-of-fact.
5. Don't underestimate how ignorant teenagers are about sex, despite their know-it-all attitude.
6. Children want to know what their parents think and believe in, even though it might not appear to be the case.

conclusion

The world of the modern teenager has changed beyond belief from our day. It is a more exciting, stimulating and dynamic place than it was for their parents thirty years ago. It has also become more complicated and there are new dangers and risks for teenagers that will require parents to be creative and better-prepared. I hope, as a result of reading this book, that you will try to praise your teenagers more. Using the 6 to 1 strategy can seem like a fruitless task because so often the teenager will appear to ignore the praise or throw it back in your face. Nevertheless, teenagers thrive on praise and, however it appears, they particularly thrive on praise from their parents. I am in no doubt that an increase in the sort of descriptive praise described in the book will lead to a decrease in bad behaviour and conflict to the extent that the whole atmosphere in the home will begin to change.

Some parents will find themselves with a hard case on their hands, where things have got really serious and they have lost control. To unravel and change a complicated behaviour pattern requires planning, organisation and real commitment in order to work. Parents must be prepared for their child to resist with all his will and there will be a real temptation to give up. There is a powerful emotional component that parents will need to be mindful of and an important part of the process is managing their own feelings and reactions. We should all remember that children need our love the most when they appear to deserve it the least.

The difficult teenage period for most children rarely lasts for more than a couple of years, though at the time it can feel like it is going on for ever. When it gets really tough, it is better to keep a thread of positive communication going than to let the relationship fall apart. This is the time for a quick loving text message or an email. Try to see the bad behaviour as a phase that will pass and keep reflecting on the many good things about your child. By hanging in there during the hardest times, parents will help their children to come out the other side when they are ready. With this help, teenagers will begin to slough off the skin of adolescence and emerge tentatively into adulthood and a new phase in the relationship between them and their parents. Parenting a teenager involves striking the balance between nurturing and letting them go and helping them bridge that gap between childhood and adulthood. Over time parents learn to make that leap of faith and say to their children, *'It's over to you now.'*

It is important for families with teenagers to continue to do things together rather than live parallel lives in the same house. Eating as a family helps to keep up these ties, particularly if parents don't focus too much on correcting their teenager's table manners. The more parents work together as a united team the easier they will find it to change their children's behaviour. Good communication between everyone in the family leads to issues being discussed and dealt with before they get out of hand.

Parents of teenagers are often carrying huge amounts of guilt, worry and anger around with them and their confidence can be rocked by what they find themselves having to deal with. Accept that it isn't all your fault when things go badly (but nor can you take all the credit when things they go well). If the book's central theme is praise, then let's have a bit of 6 to 1 for parents too.

Good luck.

index

acknowledgements

Thank you to my agent, Tif Loehnis, for her unfailing support. Thank you to the team at Vermilion, particularly Miranda West for her ideas, encouragements and enthusiasm, and to Jenny Rowley for all her help with publicity.